AF526643

The Twelve Petals of
Enlightenment

The Twelve Petals of Enlightenment

Param Hans

AUTHORSPRESS
Publishers of Scholarly Books

Worldwide Circulation through Authorspress Global Network
First Published 2011
by
Authorspress

Editorial
Q-2A Hauz Khas Enclave,
New Delhi-110 016
e-mail: authorspress@yahoo.com

Marketing
E-35/103, Jawahar Park
Laxmi Nagar, Delhi-110 092
e-mail: authorspress@yahoo.com

Copyright © 2011 Author

e-mail: gopikottoor@gmail.com

The Twelve Petals of Enlightenment
ISBN 978-81-7273-591-3

Printed in India at Tarun Offset, Delhi.

Dedicated

to

Sudarshan Kcherry

forever friend

I want to load my boat
With those waiting, thirsty ones
Who are left behind:
And carry them by the opal pool
Of iridescent joy

—*Whispers From Eternity*
Paramahansa Yogananda

The Estate of the Beautiful Mind

Are you the Enlightened one?

Enlightenment lies within each and every one of us. It flows from the inner self, in the celestial murmurs of the inner voice, and by the streams of infinite empathy. The human mind is most beautiful here. To be enlightened, we must enter our Beautiful Mind.

Think a moment of Hitler. After burning up nearly six million Jews in secret gas ovens, did Hitler become a happy man? He walked about with a cyanide capsule in his mouth everyday from day one of his war years, and ended up a depraved being, whose bitter end marks the single largest relief in the history of mankind.

The inner self works in the estate of the Beautiful Mind.

Think a moment of Mahatma Gandhi. Gandhi lived and acted for humanity by listening to his inner voice that gushed forth confidently from his Inner Self. What does the inner self really do? It works with embedded qualities that lift the heart, allowing it to bring down the ego, and flower forth with love and understanding. It cleanses the 'outer self', allowing for relaxation, rejuvenation, and peace of mind. These states amount to the happiness that we look for in our daily living.

Think of Jesus and The Buddha. They lived lives of empathy, compassion, love, and sharing. To them, personal sorrows were not as important as were the sorrows of others. Both were capable of infinite love.

They called The Buddha, 'The Enlightened One'.

What is 'Enlightenment'?

Enlightenment is but another name for being at peace with oneself. Enlightenment happens on realization, that one has entered a state where one is able to absorb pain, grief, sorrow, happiness, or even ecstasy, without disturbance to the equilibrium of being tranquil with oneself. Enlightenment stems not from detachment, but from acceptance of realities as truthful happenings within the universal order. One traverses the path when one is able to do this act without thinking of the outer self at all. Enlightenment is simple to preach, but not easy to practice. Happiness and peace are not easily attained either. But truly, the rewards in seeking enlightenment are great. Even the seeker is blessed.

You and I have specks of enlightenment floating within us.

But unlike The Buddha or Jesus, you and I do not unite all those specks to make for ourselves one wholesome beacon of lit tranquillity that we call, happiness, or peace, or by whatever name we chose to. When we learn to unite the floating specks of enlightenment within us, and succeed in uniting them, we are able to erase the outer self, or the ego. Then, the inner self made of selflessness, blossoms. This flower has all the petals of enlightenment. It is this flowering of tranquillity deep within, that dissociated Buddha from the restless Siddhartha, the prince fumbling in the dark world of sorrows and discontent.

Both The Buddha and The Christ made it possible for themselves to rise to exalted states of living by enlightening themselves, and entering their beautiful minds. They gave us this lesson of Enlightenment for us to learn from, to adapt, to make our lives happy, and let us be at peace with our selves.

This book is your stepping stone.

Step into your Beautiful Mind.

As You Open This Book of The Twelve Petals of Enlightenment...

As you open this book,
Know that your Inner Self is capable of infinite goodness.
But you haven't yet unleashed your powers for peace and tranquillity
That is infinite in its capacity
To let you be happy and in love.

This book has only one expectation from you.
Be yourself.

Go ahead and enjoy your inner self in your Beautiful Mind.
Do not be afraid to take the first step.
No one in this world is going to make you Enlightened
– But you.

Do it.
Enter your Beautiful Mind.

Contents

Petal 1
Relax

I like to call it the cat and dog mean.

Relaxation from stress, the kind you and I keep looking for, is all about the cat and dog mean. A cat on the roof is the most relaxed being. Occasionally it wakes, as though it smelt a fish or a mouse, and goes back to the relaxation mode. Unlike the dog.

The dog for that matter is for the most time excited. He is restless. Let him just see you and he sends his tail wagging as though a love comet has just been unleashed in the skies. Take him some food and he is on cloud nine. He wants to prove it, licking you through.

Where must the human being come in, if placed beside a cat and a dog? He cannot afford the extremely passive cat relaxation mode, as he has responsibilities and enough work to do. He cannot afford to be the dog either, and wear himself out. But surely, he has intellect and can learn from the calmness of the cat that keeps building on its energy levels, and he can choose the loving attitude of the dog to his master, that when translated into behaviour is pure happiness and bliss born of love and selfless thanksgiving.

Selfless happiness is joy.

By voluntarily allowing yourself to transfer your state of mind somewhere in the mean between the relaxation of the cat and the happiness of the dog, you give yourself a good chance to live in a relaxed, joyful zone of being. You are then calm.

When you truly begin to love, be it Nature, or fellow human beings, and set about to build a happy ambience around you, you give yourself inner peace. In fact, you then switch on the auto pilot of goodness, and things begin to work for you, making you feel free. You enter a state where alpha waves that help in creativity are active in your brain, helping you to be at ease with yourself. Your surroundings include not only human beings; it includes pets and other living forms as well. When you are at ease with Nature, you are calm from within. This state of well-being contributes to a state of overall contentment. No wonder that, having reached such alpha states, St. Francis of Assisi and Ramana Maharshi of Tiruvannamalai would communicate even with the birds, the squirrels, and the bees! The exalted states of relaxation and communication that they achieved were born out of love, kindness, compassion and sharing, where the outer self did not matter anymore.

To most of us, it would be worthwhile if we came to a golden mean- the centre point between the relaxed cat on the tiles and the joyful dog at the sight of its master. Being anywhere near the cat and dog mean would be an indication of being happy and relaxed. In such a state of higher contentment, there is hardly any anxiety or stress.

All stress is not bad. Positive stress at desirable levels plays functional roles on performance. This means that the rush of adrenalin is just about right, that equips you to perform to optimal levels, and thereafter you are back to normal. Positive stress helps you, for example, during your job interview, when you are getting ready to perform or are about to get started in a running race. But this is not what we usually mean when we say that someone is 'really stressed up'. When a person appears 'stressed up' his hormone situation is not within control. The person becomes a victim of his constant anxieties and fears, and he or she is unable to relax.

When stress happens to a person, the brain prepares the body to deal with an emergency. Breathing becomes rapid. Both the brain and the body are put in the defence mode. When you mess yourself up with constant fears, worries and anxieties, wrong signals are issued by the brain to the body system, which affects your health in destructive ways. The immune system that is put on hold to defend the 'emergency' comes under continual strain. Constant worry and tension can make your immune system go haywire, exposing you to infections, immunosuppressed diseases, or even cancer, apart from all the mental agony. Negative stress or undesirable stress that imbalances the mind is a potential threat to happiness and peace.

Monkeys made to undergo constant stress in laboratories have shown destructive loss of neurons in the memory encoding areas of the brain. When you worry, you are detached, anxious, distanced and all alone, brooding. You can feel your energy draining out from every pore of your being, but you think that the next step of your brooding will end it all, and that you will be happy once again. That is not true. You'll just keep holding on to your brooding thoughts and restart your worry all over again. All you get is tiredness, depression, anxiety and fatigue, with an immune system that is running you down because of your stress. Worry leads to more and more worry, and it isn't the right road to take, especially if you are looking for relaxation and contentment.

Why worry at all then? We worry because we are afraid. We doubt the existence of God, and think we are rudderless. We are afraid of failure, grief and disease, of our future and those of our loved ones, of death, and what lies after. Our reasons to worry know no end. There is no heavenly door leading to joy at the end of our worries. What do we do then at times as these?

We must learn to relax. It is important for us to be happy and in peace, here and now. What will happen later is not for us now to know or feel. But now is here for us to be happy, to be able to face the final moments of our life. We did not worry about being born, so what will happen to us after we die should not worry us by the same principle. We have two choices right in front of us. One is to worry, make our life miserable for ourselves and to die without peace of mind. The other is to be happy, to share our happiness and give ourselves and all around us peace and joy, irrespective of what sadness we might have, and to die with peace of mind. Which choice would we rather take?

Here's an experience, foremost among others, which prompted me to write this book.

I was a happy lad in my youthful days with lots of abundant energy. I wrote poetry, cycled and swam, made friends, went for picnics, but the moment I reached home, I shut myself in my room to brood over my pet anxieties and fears.

In my early twenties one day, I felt my index finger pull back and twitch. I instantly came to the conclusion that I had Parkinson's. The fasciculations that had me mad with worry and sleeplessness turned out to be a benign condition called Benign Fasciculations Syndrome or BFS. BFS had occurred to me on account of my deepening anxiety and stress. Stress and worry can set off triggers in the brain leading to twitchings, fasciculations and muscle beats, anywhere you name it, on the body. It looks embarrassing to see your muscles jerk and fingers twitch, but this happens. Unlike in Parkinson's, there is no rigidity in the muscle or slowness of movement associated with BFS. Unlike muscle dystrophies, there is no muscle loss or weakening in the EMG profiles. But BFS sure can scare you out of your wits and last for years, look like it has stopped suddenly, and come frightfully back, making you roll, worried all over again.

Worrying wasn't at all fun, but it turned out into a compulsive obsession. When I woke up, I had to worry. It was as though I needed something to worry about, to set my day going. And always, sure enough, I made up all those convincing reasons to justify my worries.

How can you apologize to yourself if you have been carrying on with twenty-three years of solid worry?

One morning in Rome, while moving past the endlessly strewn graves in the lush green Protestant cemetery, where John Keats and Shelley's heart also lie buried, I felt a sudden blur that dimmed my right eye. The fresh, colourful flowers upon the tombstones became hazy to me. By evening, the towers of the Vatican were blurred and looking dim too. I kept rubbing my eye, but the dimness did not appear to go away. Though I did not realize it then, my twenty-three years of worry had taken its toll.

I had not known what a Type A personality was, till the ophthalmologist who examined me after dilation for the distortion in my right eye with 'ocean waves' as he called it, asked me 'Are you the worrying type?', and I had not the courage to say no. 'Well, he continued, 'you have a resolved central serous retinopathy (CSR) in your right eye'. That's the reason for the line distortion in your vision, and the reason why you now see waves in straight lines. You must keep checking both your eyes on an Amsler Grid.... But don't worry, luckily, your condition is not too dangerous'.

I was stunned. My mind raced back. What had I made of myself, worrying myself to death for nothing? What is CSR doctor, I asked him. CSR he said 'is a serous discharge in the macula of the eye which is responsible for focused central vision. The macula of the eye is responsible for acuity of vision. Luckily your vision is fine. CSR most often presents in Type A personalities, who as a people are highly stressed individuals, and can never really relax. Pilots are known to get CSR for instance. The cause is not exactly known, but constant fears and stress can be major contributing factors. You must go easy on yourself for your own well-being. Don't let a relapse happen. Engage in some aerobic exercises, yoga, or relaxation techniques such as meditation and slow deep breathing.'

Well, I wondered, what had I done to myself? I had given myself only worry all these years, without relaxation of any kind. My worry had now brought me to the brink- I had not expected such an event to happen to my life. My eyes! Whatever, the CSR was now a reality, and no one was responsible for it, but me... *with my darling worries.*

What if I had started early on, trying to stretch out on my stress, relaxing myself, giving myself twenty minutes daily for meditation, or going for a twenty minute walk in the beautiful green woods near my home? What if I had adhered to the golden mean of the cat and dog principle? The CSR would never have happened to me. But, all along, I was living to myself, concerned only with one thing in my life- my worries, I decided that the important thing from now on was to get myself off imaginary worries, and try and get to where I could, to be happy.

What do you do to be Happy?

a) The golden rule to be happy is to accept yourself and move on, aspiring higher and higher. Life will put you on to extremely difficult experiences. In life's tests, the winner is he who accepts himself entirely, and goes on to his higher aspirations. The winner finds strength in change that may even appear disruptive, but uses the change to his advantage using high degrees of self-motivation.

When you next get to your bookstore, get hold of the book *Still Me* by Christopher Reeve. For those who think that life has no more meaning, because some sudden unfortunate event or change has disrupted the steady flow of life creating a blackout, *Still Me* should provide revelation and hope.

Still Me recounts in moving detail, Reeve's determined fight back into life and action, after having been paralyzed from neck down following a fall from his horse. It recapitulates how from his totally helpless condition, Reeve persevered with his inner courage and confidence to come back to independently move about in his wheel chair and even direct a major movie before his death even though every doctor attending on him had given up hope of his returning to near normal life and movement. The book reveals the real inner Superman vibrant in the heart of the actor who made the Superman comic hero a living legend in the lives of millions of children all over the world. Christopher Reeve in *Still Me* becomes the Superman for all the adults the world over. Standing tall in his wheel chair state, Reeve turns into a beacon light of inspiration for millions who need that special need of acceptance in their lives to find alternate strength in disruptive change, and to move forward.

Shakespeare was not wrong when he said 'Sweet, are the uses of adversity which, like the toad, ugly and venomous, wears yet a precious jewel in his head.' Whatever adversity does to us, our job is to find the jewel that adversity brings with it. Napoleon Hill in his best selling book '*Think And Grow Rich*' tells us that 'Adversity carries with it the seed of an equivalent or greater benefit'. Adversity spruced up King Bruce to contemplate the spider's repeated efforts to build its web, and was motivated to try again, even after he was shattered in battle and all seemed lost. He kept the little spider's efforts in mind, went on to mobilize his forces, win back his kingdom, and become king. King Bruce had in fact turned a stressed and hopeless situation into victory, because he motivated himself to handle disruptive change to his advantage.

Acceptance requires courage. When you have done all there is that you have within your means about something that's bothering your mind, and the storm still continues, that's when the power of acceptance comes in. Accept your present situation, whatever it is, with dignity. That's the noblest way to deal with your predicament. Acceptance is by no means a passive proposition. Acceptance helps you look at your problems squarely in the eye. When you accept your position, you become ready to search out alternate ways to deal with yourself. The important thing in life is to find inspiring ways to tackle the state you are in, and to move on.

The woman who brought her dead child to The Buddha, imploring him to bring her child back to life was told to fetch a mustard seed from a house that had not known death. What the Buddha wished the mother to fathom was that death was a part of life that had to be accepted as the reality of life. Acceptance of reality as a prelude to getting on with life is the moral of the parable of '*The Buddha and the Mustard Seed*'.

b) The golden rule again, to be happy, is to be thankful for what you have, and for being the one you are.

Take a good look at the photographs of the number of children, innocent and cute, appearing in newspapers because their parents need monetary support to save them from the dreaded cancer called leukemia. Or watch children in the hospital hardly able to open their eyes or suck milk, because their little muscles are dying every moment, on account of muscle degeneration. They encounter terrible pain and distress that'll hasten to snuff out their tiny lives. Stop and consider. Is your misfortune as heavy and unbearable as theirs? The children have hardly begun to cherish the value of nature, earth, love, and life. When you think of such realities, would you still think '*O my God, why only me*'? How much more human to realize, that there are deeper tragedies in this world happening to millions of innocents, by the seconds? Ask yourself this question. Are you not more fortunate in many ways than many around you?

You can be happy, when you begin to be thankful for what you have, and for being the one you are. Here is a story that will help you appreciate the heavenly values of being thankful for what you have and what you are.

A monk came into the monastery late in the night after his discourses, very tired and hungry. He called out to his favourite disciple saying 'I am so hungry I could swallow the Himalayas'. The disciple went to the kitchen but came back with his arms empty.

My master, he said 'there is no food in the kitchen. It is so late in the night and I am afraid it would be difficult now to light a fire....' The monk stood silent a moment, and murmuring to himself, 'Thank God' lay down to sleep. The disciple was baffled. The master was very hungry, there was no food in the monastery that he could eat, yet he had said 'Thank God' and laid himself peacefully down. How could that be?

The puzzled disciple went over to the master and requested him to tell him the reason for thanking God even though he was hungry, and had to retire for the night without food. The master rose, smiled and replied, 'Dear one, it is indeed true that I am hungry, and must be without food tonight. But should I not still thank God, for my appetite? Food will come to me tomorrow. I must not worry about that now. I must count myself fortunate that I have a good appetite, which I can relish on the morrow. Just think of all the people who have food before them, but cannot eat any because they have no appetite! Tell me now, am I not more graced by God than they? When I thanked God, I thanked Him for giving me a good appetite. What would I do, dear, without my appetite?'

c) Make yourself a wholesome part of the dynamic process of life and change. Live intensely, treasuring every breath of your life. Wake up to the wholesome significance of your own being.

d) Think positive. Positive thinking makes it easier for your brain to work out solutions for you in your difficult moments.

I. Here are Some Natural Ways to Relax

a) Find a quiet place

A neatly maintained part of your room with cool ventilation should be fine. Your relaxation spot could also be your favourite nook in your home garden, or a verdant shade in the woods that you might know. Close your eyes. You can then begin to move away from the thoughts that storm your mind by visualizing a flower, imagining its fragrance, or chanting a soothing word that is easy on your breath as 'OM'. You can contemplate anything serene, such as, cascading hills, verdant bloom, rain, sounds, or music that you know will soothe you and bring you peace of mind.

Slow down your breathing. Inhale gently with your stomach, and exhale slowly. Breathe from your diaphragm rather than from your chest. Diaphragmatic breathing is easy to perform. It helps lower your blood pressure and is healthy for your lungs and heart.

Be in the relaxation mode for as long as you wish to be.

b) Have pets in your home

Behavioural scientists and analysts swear by the good effects of keeping pets in the house. There's nothing like a loving puppy that can lick you away to elated states of calm and happiness. Having pets, cuddling them, talking to them, and giving them love is the closest you can get to happiness, if you can't get across to touch and cuddle your loved ones or do not have any. If you don't have pets, create an imaginary aquarium in your mind, with varieties of exotic coloured fish swimming in them. Imagination is the limit.

c) Order an aquarium in your workroom or office

Aquariums work wonders to calm a troubled mind. Letting your eyes wander with the graceful movements of pets in the aquarium helps produce a sense of inner calm. This is especially true if you are prone to hypertension in the workplace, or are recovering from a heart or brain stroke.

d) Keep touching your loved ones

Touch is a great healer of distress. Touch is electric and takes you to heights of love and happiness. Hug your loved ones. Start today. Just go over and hug your loved ones over and over. Feel the change instantly. It is easy. Once you start the *touch- and-stay-in-touch* principle, you'll find how easy it is not to let go. Go ahead. Keep in touch.

e) Be playful

Being with children, playing with them wholeheartedly, reading story books to them, or simply conversing with them offer great possibilities to get yourself down and relax. Make an appointment with a childrens' group manager close to your town and say you would like to spend time with the children in that organization. Take sweets to them, watch for their birthdays, play and share their little joys that'll help to drown your own sorrows and states of stress or depression. Go to a society for autistic or spastic children, and take part in their happiness. See what you can do for at least one of them. Such activities help make life peaceful and meaningful.

f) ***Laugh and cry***

Do not hold up your emotions and let them wreck you from within. Do not allow yourself to suppress grief inside you in ways that'll make you bleed and implode. Laugh and cry. No one else is as interested in your happiness and peace of mind as you are. Laughter and tears are great emotional relaxants. Make active use of your laughter and tears.

g) *Pray together*

Praying together brings the family closer. You don't really even have to believe in God or ask of Him favours. If your family believes in prayer, just join them, because you belong to your family and they need you just as you need them. Pray for nothing, but just for the inner strength to be happy together. Tell yourself in your prayer that you'll make happiness possible for yourself and your family. It is an old dictum, but also a great message that the family that prays together, stays together.

h) *Walk alone in the woods*

Find a serene pathway for yourself in the nearby woods where you can have communion with nature- the sounds of rustling leaves or the tranquility of the mountain falls. Walk with a mantra (the mantra could even be your daughter's name!) on your lips. Walk in the early mornings, or just at about sunset when the beach is in tranquill twilight. If you don't have a comfortable mantra, then think of the things you did to make others happy in the recent past, with your smile, your polite gesture, or your little acts act of compassion, encouragement and kindness. Think of how much you could empathize during the day. Think of all those moments when you missed out on being human or lost control of yourself, bringing anxiety and unhappiness to yourself.

i) Keep talking to your mind

Remember, that there is a faithful friend sitting in your heart, waiting to make you happy, if only you will listen to him. Make it a point to make frequent visits to your heart to talk with your inner friend. Consult him in times of trouble, or whenever you might need help, and pay heed. You may, even engage in silent conversations with your inner voice, while you are on your way to work, or even jetting across in an airplane. At such times, switch off your cell phone or lap top, and just be on the same wave length with your inner voice. When you get the instinctive feel of those right answers for your problems, accept them and go ahead..

j) Reinforce strategies to accept your pain, your disease, your discomforts and find ways to see the positive side of the position you are in

Every cloud has a silver lining, however dark it might be. Find out that silver lining in your dark cloud, and move forward.

k) Pay close attention to everything that you see, feel, touch, or hear.

Do not take things for granted. Look deep into nature and art with a probing, reflective eye. Bring out the power in your mind's eye, and see and hear for yourself, the treasures of nature and art that you so long took for granted.

l) Have a keen eye for beauty all around you

Enjoy beauty all around you now as though you'll never see it again.

m) Attempt to study people by interacting with them and try to understand the dynamics of human behaviour

Have a pleasant attitude when interacting with people. Be appreciative, and try to collect friendships, whenever, and wherever you are. Being with friends helps you tide away your worries. When in company, do not try to get joy at somebody's expense or by hurting somebody. Laughter gained at the expense of your friend, or by causing hurt or pain to someone isn't really worth it.

n) Behave with people in a manner that'll help you to be remembered by them long after you are gone from their side

That is the about the best attitude to life and relationships that you can develop as a human being. When you are away, let them say about you 'He was a genuine human being.' By being polite and giving respect, you can live anywhere, with anyone, and make yourself happy, wherever you are.

o) Cut out negatives such as 'I am unworthy' or 'I am unwanted'. Instead, turn negatives into positives

Look without, with self-confidence from within. Come up with a list of things that you know you are really good for, and are capable of. Work on them to your advantage. Avoid self-pity. Avoid being pessimistic.

p) Adapt

Accepting life situations and winning in life, is nearly all about being flexible. A bend in the road of life may look sharp and dangerous, but can present you with magnificent scenery which you otherwise might have not even have noticed. Life is all about bends, accepting new pastures, and tilling the new soil if it is rough, to let it bear fruits for you. Happiness in life begins with what we do with the changes it presents ourselves with, and by tapping its brighter side and hidden possibilities.

q) The key to survival is restrained flexibility

Those who evince 'Restrained Flexibility' continue to be effective in a suddenly changed environment. And just how do they do it? By being strong enough to bend over when the storm blows through them, and coming back unscathed, after the storm has gone. Think of the tall, magnificent trees. They were there with our forefathers, they are here with us today, and will live to seen by our great grandchildren and beyond. How? Because they let the storm and the cyclone pass them by, bending to let the obstacles pass, and are back to their upright selves again. The millions of species that exist today are there with us because they were able to adapt to evolutionary changes. Those that could not adapt, even though big and strong like the dinosaurs, failed to make it through the evolutionary process. The rule is simple. Adapt and survive.

r) Keep your aims and goals in focus

Remember that it isn't your ego that is more important than your attitudes and your goals in life. Keep working towards goals, while allowing yourself relaxation and peace.

s) Snap that work continuum wherever you are

Wherever you are, or whenever you feel your work turning complicated, go for short intermittent interludes by closing your eyes, and taking slow deep breaths. Open your eyes and get back to your work.

t) Discuss your worry with loved ones

Most often a favourable response by the ones who love you and care for you helps you to shed your worries. It is important to have someone you have faith in, to get to listen to your worries, even if he or she is there just to there to lend you an ear. If you have a health problem that's worrying you, check it out with your doctor, do the necessary tests, and get it over with. The important thing to get done is to get out of your stress box early and quickly. If it is a family problem that concerns you, talk it over with your family. Don't let your worry wreck you from within.

u) Got a problem with your kid?

Take him out with you, and talk with him. Listen to his problem as you would to a friend. Make him feel that he can trust you enough to make you his confidant.

II. Here are Some Attitudinal Boosters that'll Help Turn Your Life Around

a) Forgive and forget, naturally. Do not nurse old wounds or harbour hatred.

b) Be Humble. Enjoy being humble to yourself, and to those around you.

c) Empathize and Sympathize. Resolve to do more and more good others.

d) Accept constructive criticism. Look inward to see if you can learn from the attitudes and views of others towards you. Do not feel ashamed to correct yourself.

e) Do not blame anyone for what's happening to you. Worry and blame are of the same brotherhood. Don't worry, and don't blame others.

f) Boost your self-esteem. Keep and enjoy a healthy lifestyle.

g) Accept responsibility with an open mind. Be open and transparent.

h) Make active sex a part of your love life. Good loving sex contributes to a life of health, and restores your love life.

i) Develop the art of being patient. Being patient and calm supports you during times of anger. Go slow when tense or angry. Take time to give yourself slow deep breaths, exhaling, and counting to ten, to let your negative stress pass by.

j) Go visually creative. Feed your mind often with deeply enriched visual imagery. It promotes alpha waves that contribute to your creativity, and act to embalm the mind to good effect.

k) Find friends with common areas of interest. Get active, and interact with likeminded friends to bring out the positive traits in you. They help you relax. Interested in poetry? Join a poetry club, or make one yourself and for fellow poets, and read and discuss poems. Spend time creatively and reap your rewards.

l) Be spontaneous. Get natural. Be quick to understand and respect the freedom of those around you. Do not be rigid in your daily actions or behaviour. Do not let life's little irritants bother you. Learn, if they offer lessons to you, or go easy over them as you feel them coming, without letting them upset you in any manner.

m) Practice non -violence. Practice non-violence as a way of life.

n) Tread softly. Try not to enter into situations that'll make you repent, or feel guilty later.

III. And While You Retrospect

a) *Listen to your body rhythms.* Ask yourself to find out whether you are listening to your mind and body rhythms. Try and make peace with your bio rhythms. Are you a day person?

Or do you work better after everyone has gone to sleep? Are you an owl? Get the maximum out of yourself by listening to your own mind and body needs. If you are creative after 10.00 p.m., go ahead and work or paint in your study after ten in the night. Or do you like to rise early and do your homework? Ask yourself what best suits you to get you the maximum from yourself in terms of fulfillment.

b) *Do your Kegel anytime, anywhere.* Do you feel like doing Kegel exercises right in the middle of a crowded lift? Go ahead and do them. No one will know, but certainly you'll benefit, and be relaxed and healthy.

c) *Write your happiness book.* Write a home journal, travel book, or your observations about interesting people or places you have come across. Explore spaces and characters, and relive them in your mind for memories and nostalgia. Such actions refresh memory, boost creativity, and augment cognition.

d.) *Develop your Emotional Quotient.* Some of the most successful and happy people are those who possess energized Emotional Quotient (EQ). Emotional Quotient has everything to do with empathy, awareness and helpful attitudes. People who empathize are good listeners, and are happy to tackle the problems of others as well. Their EQ lets them find quick practical solutions where higher IQ minds have floundered. Persons with high EQs makes good team leaders and efficient crisis managers as well.

e) *Fill your emotional treasury.* Follow your emotional behaviour in ways that can make you helpful to children, relatives, family and friends. When people around you see you as a helpful person, you get to be loved more and more, which can add to your emotional treasury. You are encouraged in the process to transcend yourself.

f) *Make a list of the qualities that you know you have.* Look at people around you. Give yourself points for the happiness and relaxation you have brought upon yourself and for others. Did your acts of sharing, giving respect, being helpful and calm, offer you inner relaxation? Could you rejoice in the success of your friend without feeling envy? Think of all the jealous thoughts about your friends that you were able to strike out from your mind. How many such negative thoughts could you knock off from your mind by the day's end? Could you fill your mind with thoughts of compassion and of ways you could help your friends by trying to understand their difficulties? How many such ways to forgive and forget, and restart relationships over again without nursing hurts and wounds, could you manage by the day's end? What positive impact did they have on you? Did they make you feel better and peaceful at heart?

IV. Help Yourself to be Happy

Learn to be kind, attentive, and responsible to your body and mind. You end up being a better and balanced human being by energizing your inner reserves to attain peace and relaxation. You certainly want to give up certain habits that you know, stand in the way of your pursuit of happiness.

a) Give up smoking, and the use of all forms of tobacco. Contrary to the theories promoted by smokers with tar and nicotine in their lungs and mouths, smoking never made anyone on earth happy. Every puff of a cigarette adds to craving and restlessness, increases anxiety, thickens blood vessels, and increases workloads for the heart and lungs. Whenever you have the urge to smoke, think of the Malboro cowboy who spent the younger part of his life advertising the cowboy brand of cigarettes, and the later part of life campaigning against cigarette smoking, while going down with lung cancer.

Here are a few tips to help you quit smoking.

Quit now. Throw away that packet in your pocket. Don't even think about it. The best way to give up the tobacco habit is to quit instantly. Keep asking yourself what joy you get inhaling carbon, rolled paper and tar. What joy is there in having ulcers turning to cancer in your mouth and lungs? Tear open your cigarette roll after the first few puffs and look at the dust and sediments inside. Feel for yourself the wet sticky tar that starts forming, looking like ear wax. Imagine how they get sticky inside your lungs that are otherwise clear as a new born cotton cloud, and tender as silk. Never smoke more than the first two or three puffs of your newly lit cigarette, if you have to smoke. As you continue to smoke your cigarette, you let more and more of the carcinogenic toxins, resin, and tar sticking along the residual length of your cigarette enter and work havoc in your mouth, throat, respiratory fields, and lungs. Keep thinking of your dear and loved ones, and what it would mean to you and to them if you derailed yourself, smoking. You know you'll make your children happy if you don't smoke. Make a small sacrifice for others near you that'll in turn do you good. Turn around and listen to your inner voice before it gets too late. Just don't smoke.

b) *Say no to drugs.* Your 'no' to drugs should be firm as a rock. Do not use hard drugs as heroin, opium, cocaine, LSD, or Ecstasy. Say no to all forms of street drugs. Do not self-medicate with tranquilizers, sedatives or amphetamines. Do not be tempted to use anabolic substances and steroidal formulations as the consequences of their use without medical guidance can prove to be fatal.

c) *Do not engage in alcohol abuse.* Drink only if you must, and that too, strictly in moderation. Alcohol is a not a relaxant. In fact, it really is a depressant. The more you consume alcohol wanting to be happy and in high spirits, the more sad and depressed you'll become. An initial high soon wears away, and you are then worn down completely. Taking alcohol (ethyl alcohol) in large doses leads to interference with liver function. The liver must stop all its natural work to deal with alcohol to filter the toxin on top priority basis. Alcohol also interferes with absorption of vital vitamins useful for balanced functioning of the entire system. Its abuse can lead to a variety of problems with the liver, the kidneys, the eyes, and the brain, that could prove permanent or fatal. But there is indeed a silver lining if you stick to moderation. Scientists believe that alcohol in moderation i.e., one to two standard drinks a day of about 45- 90 ml. of liquor, the likes of whiskey, brandy or rum, a medium bottle of beer, or a standard glass of wine, can provide beneficial effects both on physical and mental health. However, considering the risks of addiction and abuse involved in alcohol consumption, nondrinkers are advised not to start alcohol intake just for the sake of the benefits of moderate intake. Thirty minutes of brisk walking or mild aerobic exercises daily work better wonders, both for relaxation as well as for the heart! Binge drinking is not recommended for relaxation.

V. And ...

Open your happiness cum relaxation diary. Make it a point to make entries every day before you retire to bed. Note the good things you did that instantly made you happy and relaxed. Recollect the efforts you made to make others happy, and to get along with people. Give yourself bonus points for the efforts you made to control your anger, and to make peace with yourself. Did you lend a helping hand to someone not as fortunate as you? Did you speak lovingly to your wife and children more often?

Let your happiness diary be a creative book. Fill your diary with observations from nature. Sketch the flowers that you saw, the colours that you cherished, the hills you trekked, the people you met, the landscapes you loved... . On weekends, read through your week day deeds and take a retrospective of yourself. Were you not moved to write poems? If so did you write them? Did you do everything you could for your own happiness by giving faith a chance, and with the best of intentions, to make others happy?

Make your happiness diary your treasure chest. As you write your book, you'll be astonished that you have so much potential to make true happiness and peace possible for yourself. You will be astonished at your own powers of observation and surprised too, at the surging forth of creativity that lay so long dormant within you. Treasure your happiness diary, because it is the book of your heart, and the only one of its kind in the world.

Be at home in your Beautiful Mind.

Petal 2
The Lotuses in the Lake

Think of the times you wanted to talk to the person next to you in the train or in the cinema queue, or to the passenger beside you on the air plane, but refrained from doing so, hoping perhaps that the 'other' would make the first move. Who knows how many real friendships you may have missed out on, with opportunities totally gone, because you did not take that first step. It is strange but true, that some of the best friends were made by that snap talk and the first move someone made, which got around to last a lifetime.

The need to talk and express ourselves is a basic human need. Even while we are in thoughts, we engage ourselves in a silent talk process. We in fact need to keep talking to reach out and value our own emotions and ourselves. We cannot do that to the four walls. When we are anxious or restless, we even talk in our sleep! We cry out loud to no one in particular, wanting the world to hear us and sympathize with us, when our grief turns inconsolable. It is only by talking and showing our expressions that we are able to be really human, and remain so. Our bitter silences are those that are forced upon us. Communication bonds help release our tension, and enable us to attain and maintain levels of calm.

To shut the door on the face of friends, or the society we live in, is to force upon ourselves mental execution. Independent living, though desirable, must not be confused with self withdrawal or isolation. True to the adage, *no man is an island.* A pleasing greeting from your side, a smiling hello, or an invitation to converse should help reveal in a second or two, if the person with whom you would communicate, is interested in being your friend. If the initial response is fine, you may begin by showing your interest in the person, and invite him to an open dialogue. An open dialogue does not take a mere 'Yes' or 'no' as a response. If the initial communication looks good for both of you, you may exchange cards or e mail addresses that will later help to further bond your contact into mutual friendship. Do not be afraid to ask for visiting cards or e mail ids. But when you do so, be polite to offer your card or id first just as you should begin a meaningful conversation by first revealing your identity. In fact, one of the best ways to be an extrovert and optimist is to meet people, get to talk with them, and exchange ideas. Do not keep ulterior ends in view when you start to have a friendship. Be natural. Who knows, such contacts may even help build careers or elevate one's own prospects in life.

Make yourself happy to be with people. Talking and listening to people make for great joys of life. It is all the more joyous to have people around you who share your interests and attitudes. The act of being with friends helps shed inhibitions. It promotes a feeling of well-being, and of acceptance, which is desirable.

Be genuinely interested in the interactions you initiate. Set yourself to tune into the game of understanding people, and the manner in which they expend their emotions. By your interactive mode, you get to learn more about the psychology of human behaviour which in itself is a fascinating science. Make learning human behaviour your forte.

When getting around to linking with people, you learn to put to test your own strengths and weaknesses as a human being, and to adapt and be flexible. You learn the value of building friendships, and the art of treading softly on others' dreams. In the process you get to be a better empathizer and sympathizer. You expand life's horizons for yourself, and virtually gain in the process.

People generally tend to be withdrawn to themselves. As Thoreau noted, the mass of men lead lives of desperate quiet. It is this desperation that drives people to be defensive and offensive by first reactions. You'll find that if you interact politely and genially with people, they are also quick to shed their defences, their inhibiting egos, and would like to become friends with you.

When dealing with people, and taking the first step in doing so, remember that you are trying out experiments in interactive behaviour. All the more reason for you to tread carefully. Many a time, you must be prepared to crack a hard nut to feel its soft insides. There are times it could hurt you. That is when you should be able to control your rising ego and focus on your goal. Not all your trials will be successful. When you dig for treasure, you must be prepared to hit rocks, if you want to get your diamonds. Keep the faith. Keep digging for the benefit of enriched relationships out of strangers, for life.

The minds of people operate on various levels based on their personal experiences in life, and how they think life has treated them. Unlike you, many with whom you interact do not even realize that they should take charge of their own lives to make themselves happy.

When The Buddha attained Enlightenment he was really in a fix. What would he do with the great power of Enlightenment that he had attained? How would he be able to percolate it down to the common man? Unless Enlightenment benefited mankind, of what was 'The Awakening'? As he walked on, he came to a large lake with many lotuses in them. Seated by it in contemplation, he observed, that though there were many lotuses in the lake, they were all there in various stages of their blossoming. Some of them were yet buds. Some of the buds lay half open, and submerged under the water. A few of the lotuses however stood bright and tall, ready to receive upon their red petals, the brightening radiance of the morning sun. Watching the lotus flowers in various stages of their bloom, The Buddha intuitively realized its message for him, and he felt himself ready to spread the message of 'The Enlightenment' among his people. He knew that it would be easier for him to begin his sermon among those that were learned among men, who had attained a sense of stature, just as the few lotuses that stood well above the water, ready to absorb the radiance of the sun. They in turn would percolate his message to those around them, and so on, and so forth.

We are all like the lotuses in the lake. We remain in varying degrees of our growths at the various stages of our lives. Most of us do not even give a second thought about looking within ourselves, or of listening to our inner voice, to let happiness and peace all around us.

We are mostly looking for our happiness through someone else's looking glass. Husbands think that their wives ought to make them happy; the wives think that their husbands ought to do that. Often we hear the words 'He doesn't make me happy' when we would rather hear 'I want to make him happy'. In your office your boss is not happy, and he wants you to please him and make him happy. Wherever we go, we find that it is in our human nature to keep passing on our 'Happiness baby' as though somebody else ought to be responsible for our happiness. We seem to believe that our responsibility ends with seeking or demanding our own happiness from somebody else. All our life, we get around with an invisible board on our backs which says '*Make me happy*'. It never happens. We search happiness in the wrong places and virtually never find it. We continue to remain unhappy all our lives.

No one said it better than the poet saint Tulsidas who compared man's blind search for God everywhere except within, as akin to the musk deer that keeps searching the entire forest for musk, not aware that it holds the musk sac within itself.

Help yourself find that happiness within you, and spread it around for others less fortunate than you are. That is the way to operate the 'Holistic Happiness Principle'. You operate from within. You get yourself to move around, lighting happiness outside you, everywhere, and being happy, from within.

A person who sat next to me in a train introduced himself and we got talking. He said he had recently changed his job and landed as a media controller in a Swiss bank branch and was going for training in Basel within a fortnight. The next part of what he said about how he landed in the Swiss bank was pleasantly surprising. He was alone in the lift one day going up to his office as usual where he worked as a clerk, when a lady entered the lift from the fifth floor. For a while they were quiet. On an impulse, my friend then wished the lady good morning. The lady was pleasantly surprised that a total stranger should warmly wish her so, and she was again impressed with his pleasing qualities of initiating a conversation and keeping it going. They exchanged their cards. Imagine my friend's surprise when he got a letter home one day from her bank in Switzerland where the lady was the corporate head, saying that they were wondering if he would join them as a media controller and public relations officer and that he could state his willingness by return fax! Imagine that. Just a 'Good morning' bringing in a fortune!

Have genuine interest in people. Do not measure size while interacting. Remember that inside each one, the size of the human heart is just about the same. Life is all about meeting people and staying in touch.

During journeys, if a person shows interest in you, and wishes to engage in conversation, find ways to continue the conversation from your side in a meaningful way. Find areas of mutual interest to keep your conversation on. Take care not to lose e-mails or cards you might get, or make a special folder to record details of the acquaintances you make. Periodically renew your contacts. We must practice the art of following up our acquaintances and keeping our contacts alive, as each contact has definite possibilities.

When one wishes to engage in conversation, one must take special care to open up one's body language. It is necessary to keep one's eyes and ears open, and to smile, making eye contact while doing so. Sitting cross legged or with crossed arms is taken to be a sign of negative response that prevents meaningful associations. Saying hello and getting beyond needs a lot of grit. But by doing so, the field is yours to conquer.

Do not take pride in being known as 'One who is reserved'. There is no off beat glory in that statement. By communicating, you lose nothing. In fact you gain that which you would have lost, had you not talked. Make your moves right, create the friends you need, understand strangers and make them your friends. Delete the odd ones who do not vibe with you. It is easy. In the game you play making new friends, try and come up winning.

One day an old time friend stopped me and asked 'Do you know where I'd been to?' Well, I didn't. 'I was in Florida, and I also visited the Grand Canyon.'

'Oh, you did?'

'Well, it was a chance meeting. He was a tourist and looking for a good place to stay. I offered him a free room in my home near the beach and he was thrilled. He stayed with us and we became good friends. Imagine, he went back to the States, asked me to get my passport, as he was sending me a sponsorship for a visit to America. All too quick! Well, that is the story of my visiting the White House, Walt Disney, and The Grand Canyon!'

My friend hadn't really expected an invitation to the States when he offered his help to the American tourist. But it happened that way. As a rule, do not make friendships with mean and selfish motives in view. That is the golden part of learning to be friends with those you might encounter. Sometimes your new friend may need your help. If his need is genuine, do not back out. Let the friendships you create be natural and spontaneous. The rest will follow.

Here is another true story that I'll never forget.

A friend of mine, a salesman in an ad-hoc company, kept nursing his dream of manufacturing a new type of printing press with his innovative technique for which a patent was pending. He was one of seven children, and had to give away his pay for his father's treatment every month. He was in very dire straits.

He used to commute every day by train. One evening he sat opposite a tall handsome stranger. Being an extrovert by nature he introduced himself, and the two of them got talking. Somewhere along the talk-line my friend mentioned to him about his innovation and his dream to make the printing press project a reality. It happened that the stranger was a scientist, a wealthy man who held a key post in the government service. The idea looked good to the stranger as he heard it, and so he gave my friend his address and asked him to contact him so they could talk further in the matter.

Well, to cut a long story short, the scientist helped my friend to get his patent, and himself resigned from his work to devote himself to helping my friend to set up his project, by taking on a position as advisor in a company that they registered together. They bought a piece of land from the Government that had been designated as for industrial promotion. Within two years the company rolled out the first printing press which my friend had never imagined he would make except in his dreams! Business began to pick up steadily, and the orders for the new press began to go international. In ten years, my friend made it to the top ten business entrepreneurs in the country. He went on to win the President's medal for 'Excellence in Business Entrepreneurship'. Today in the twelfth year of having met his benefactor, my friend is the Chairman of his company, Intimate Technologies, which markets its brand of printing presses across the world. Today my friend is a globe trotter. Whenever I ring him on his mobile, he says hello from somewhere over the Atlantic or the Caribbean while flying to meet his market. How did all that happen? Simply, because my friend as a person also had a high degree of interactive capacity along with his talent for innovation, and he was always genuinely interested in people. What if he had kept his mouth shut in the train in front of the stranger? Well, he would still be selling biscuits by street shop windows. But that is not the end of my friend's story. His is the only company in leftist driven Kerala that boasts of not having had a single labour episode since inception, which again speaks volumes for his interactive power to build up his relationships to business advantage.

One day, while taking me on a rail tour of his company my friend confided to me that even though he was the CEO of Intimate Technologies, he did not even keep a room for himself with a banner. Moving around, I saw that what he said was true. There was no room bearing the banner of the CEO in the entire five-acre company and factory complex. He was always around assisting his labourers or staff. He was always on the rounds and took his rest when tired, in a chair in the big conference room of the office. He initiated welfare measures that included cooperatives that allowed subsidized food for his staff. He formulated for them a highly acclaimed cooperative insurance plan. True to his words he was part of the big company and not its superman in a flash coat and tie. My friend's reason for his steadfast success was indeed because he was committed to the welfare of the people who worked for him, because he genuinely cared for them.

It is part of the Holistic Happiness Principle that you make others happy, and they give you happiness and room for you to succeed, letting happiness in turn, work for you. My friend has even gone beyond implementing welfare measures for the staff members of his company. Every year he prints text books from his press for the poor children in town and distributes them free of costs to the Government schools. He shares his birthday with children whose parents are in prison, or with inmates in the home of the mentally challenged, distributing toffee and cakes to them and partaking of their joy and happiness. Here is a true man, a multi-faceted genius with outstanding E.Q, a lotus above the waters, who knows to breathe in the fragrance of the flower of enlightenment!

I was once flying home from Texas, where I was teaching creative writing and English to freshmen at the Texas State University. A polite German mathematician who boarded the plane from Brussels came over, smiled, and sat next to me. There was good wine being served and a bad film on the screen in front of us, and we soon got talking. The gentleman told me that he was a mathematician by profession, but that his special interests lay in reading poetry and painting. He said he was on his way to India to deliver a mathematical lecture. I told him that I wrote poetry and had a website where he could read some of the poetry that I had posted. He agreed and we exchanged e-mail ids before parting.

Early one morning while looking up my emails I found my friends mail asking how I'd been. We became e mail friends. I was fascinated by my friend's deep love for literature and painting. He sent me an antique edition of Shakespeare's 'Midsummer Night's Dream' in German translation, and I sent him my poem 'Father, Wake Us In Passing' that I had written at my father's bedside at the time of his terminal coma. My poem sequence had received critical appreciation in literary circles and some rare touching reviews to add, and so, I thought it worthwhile to send it to him. My friend wrote to me that he liked the poem sequence a great deal. He showed it to a German publisher who had it translated into German and published in Germany as a sleek, beautiful English- German poetry booklet. The book won me an invitation to be Poet-in-Residence in Augsburg University where I read out the poem along with my translator and publisher. Thereafter I conducted readings of the poem sequence on invitation in various universities across Germany.

When I look back wondering how it all happened, I must accept that the readings in Germany would not have happened had we not become friends that late evening during our flight to India together. Our friendship for life happened just because the two of us seated side by side one evening in the plane, laughed and became friends for sheer joy. Just because the two of us, though total strangers until then, smiled, believed in each other, got talking and became brothers in the sky, for life!

There are people waiting to be our friends-you'll find them everywhere, if only you are willing to give friendship a real try. When we start showing genuine interest in people, our luck, our fortunes and sometimes even our future, begins to change. When we win friends over to us, we get the power to get ahead in life. Above all, friendship gives us the power to realign our lives to new priorities and opportunities. New friendships make for new forms of happiness.

When we show real interest in people, we attract them to us. People everywhere are looking for a little faith and understanding. When we offer them our understanding, they are willing to shed their ego and walk the mile to help us. For most people, the ego is a wall created by them out of lack of confidence in themselves. By creating friends, we transcend such artificially built walls laden with anxiety, and other forms of latent insecurity.

Let our words be gentle and our body language open. That's the best way to bring people around to help us and to bond with us.

How to Make Friends the Natural Way

a) Go ahead and play the game of making friends. Add to your list friend list every day. Make friends with your doctor, the nurse, the film operator, the care-taker, the student, and the under-taker. Make no reservations, just talk and make friends.

b) Make a list of the friends you make. List out their contact ids. Make it your favourite home work.

c) Shut out your mobile phone and talk to the person next to you for a change. Who knows, you may have a good friend waiting.

d) Be genuine in your love of people.

e) Show your love and concern. Learn to comfort and console as your build your friendships. Teach your friends to look for the brighter side of things.

f) Remember birthdays of friends and show them that you remember.

g) Take that first step to make friends. Why fear when there is nothing to lose and perhaps, everything to gain?

h) Work to build bridges between human beings. Bridges that'll help to see one another through.

Just how do you interact with people, get talking, and keep talking?

a) Be pleasant to be with.

b) Say hello. Hello is a magic word to begin an interaction. When Alexander Graham Bell invented the telephone, 'Hello' was the word that he spoke into the mouthpiece of the new invention he had made— and the word has stuck as the starting point for most conversations, for most love affairs in the world, and as the start-up word in almost every interaction between two strangers- ever since. Say hello with a smile, or with an attitude which shows willingness to go further than just a Hello.

c) Ask questions that'll require extended replies rather than an abrupt shaking of the head in response, or a 'yes' or 'no'. For example, if you are in a theatre queue and you wish to talk to the one in front of you, imagine the reply if you ask him 'Is there another show after this? He might as well nod his head, or reply 'Yes' or "No'. But if you ask him what he thinks of the theatre performance or about a particular actor's role, he cannot say yes, or no, he must give his views. That is a thread from where you can pull him towards you and get the talking started, going into deeper issues in the opera, and getting to know his attitudes better. As you get talking, and obtaining his views, try to enter the person's mind.

d.) Your body language is important while attempting a conversation. Be open in body gestures to make the other person comfortable while interacting with you.

e) Create conditions that are favourable for you to interact. You may, if you want to strengthen your interactive levels, invite your new friend over to a cafe or take an appointment from him for a later date and time to dwell further on issues of common interest you may have discussed together.

f) If you find a person difficult to get along with, you must make your choices whether you wish to continue the acquaintance or not. It would be well to remember the famous example by which Stephen. R. Covey explained 'The Paradigm Shift'. Covey in his book 'The Seven Habits Of Highly Successful People' tells us how our responses to a person's behaviour which we perceive as irrational or unnatural undergoes a change and shift the moment we recognize and understand the reason for such behaviour. A person's behaviour is basically characterized by his experiences good or bad, his responses to moods, or the way life situations have treated him. Most of the time we look for idealized responses from others which we seldom get, because people's behaviour are by and far connected to their own experiences, or are defences they put forward. A keen observer of human behaviour must be able to express understanding, and enter the 'feelings' of others in order to achieve his aim of winning him over to his side.

g) If people get angry at you, it is necessary and vital not to counter the feelings in the same manner. A pause in between while you allow yourself to breathe slow, also lets the other person settle and calm down.

h) Try and rate your own ability to interact with people and try out streaks that you find are helpful to win people over to your side. This can be fun and you don't have to bend down low or stoop to conquer.

i) Have some jokes ready, some quotes, to share and visibly impress. Subjects such as films and sports are lively to start with and keep the conversation going for a while. Make a good impression with your polite attitude, gentle behaviour and use the qualities to build on a foundation of trust.

j) Show that you value the friendship you just made. After taking the first step, stay in touch. Unlike in the past, e-mail makes it so easy to keep communication alive. Make maximum use of e-mail opportunities to be interactive.

k) Learn from Nature. We all love things that look pleasant. Look at the smile upon a dolphin's face. We are instantly attracted to it. See the puppy in the street. Before it becomes a ferocious dog that snarls and bites, it is all there for you, taking the first step, wagging that little tail and willing to walk the rest of the way with you. You are instantly attracted to it. In all its spontaneity, the puppy has taken the first step to offer your delight! Isn't it strange that all the riches in this world cannot make you happy, but a puppy in the street looking at you with happiness on its face and wagging its silly tail expressing its pleasure at seeing you, can? If you are happy and pleasant, you'll draw people towards you. Everyone likes to be with a gregarious person, because he is a great motivator of people and contributes to the Holistic Happiness Principle.

And ...

Your actions of good will determine how you'll be treated by others. Let your mind be like the puppy or the dolphin. Let your love for all whom you meet be natural, full of happiness, and true.

Talk your way through your Beautiful Mind.

Petal 3

Turn Your Life Around

The story of the man with the salt biscuits, the priest and the children, and other stories.

One evening a seventy year (or more) old man sat beside me in the bus on my way home. Three children, all below twelve, sat opposite him. I could see that one of them was really famished, and looking very hungry too.

The elderly man, who wore a collar to protect his neck, took out a packet of biscuits from his suitcase. He then fished out his newspaper. Perhaps it was the sound of the wrapper or the sudden fragrance of biscuits in the air that made the three children turn around and stare at the man with four biscuits in his hand all of which he popped at once into his mouth oblivious of his surroundings, with the children staring at him, their tiny mouths open.

Imagine that. A man of seventy years or more did not have the courtesy or the kindness, nay not even the thought to offer at least one salt biscuit to the children before him. I watched the three little children stare at the big grandpa digging into the four biscuits like an aged carnivore, and it left me wondering where the elderly man's sense of sharing had vanished. Had his seventy years or more on earth brought him down only to this? How much better it would have felt for his aged heart, if he had cared to offer a biscuit to the children seated before him?

The episode took me back to a painting I had seen in my childhood depicting Sir Philip Sidney, the Elizabethan soldier-poet being carried in a stretcher, fatally wounded, giving away his water-bottle to another wounded soldier saying '*Thy need is yet greater than mine*'.

What if the old man had offered his biscuits to the children in front of him? There would have been four happy faces munching away in delight! A little bit of sharing would have gone a long way, bringing a sense of well-being all around.

Let us move on to another story.

I'll always remember the aged priest of our local church with love and awe. He was a solitary man. Every time that he came down to our street (which he always did on Sundays after Mass) children from all over suddenly crowded around him like swift bees. From his pocket, the priest used to bring up small toys, coloured ribbons, sugar candy and chocolates which he gave away to the kids swarming him as he walked on. The priest was also seventy years or more.

Now look at the two people. The first one was closed, and he kept to himself. He did not seem to care for sharing, and was unaware of the happiness that would have been his, had he shared his biscuits with the children seated before him. The priest, on the other hand, laughed and played with the children, and brought joy to himself and happiness to the kids around him.

Both were senior citizens, old men riding their chariots of time towards heaven, but in what different ways! One was cold, rigid, and tense, unmindful of the world around him, while the other was open to his surroundings, spreading love around him, sharing and caring, as he moved on. The priest was indeed rooted in the world, but moved in love, lighting candles of joy. Now, who among them was happy and why?

There is all the happiness in sharing. True sharing cannot come about without genuine affection and love for those around us. Those who have a sense of sharing are open, aware of their surroundings, and observant of those around them. The act of sharing leads them to care. Such sharing has benevolent effects on one's heart which pays in the form of happiness.

Here are a few stepping stones you can climb to share, and be happy.

a) Find joy in giving. Buy sweets on your way home. Give them away to the children you meet while going to work. Give them away with a smile.

b) Spend time sharing love and laughter with friends whom you trust.

c) Share quality time with loved ones. Keep family conversations on. Bring fun and laughter back into the family.

d.) Give for the joy of giving, and for the sense of sharing, and thereafter forget.

e) Think not while you give away that you are giving away to someone of lesser worth. Think of yourself as the beggar. Would the coin that someone flipped at you give you enough to buy yourself a cup of coffee or a square meal? When you give away, give with warmth in your heart and in ways that'll satisfy basic human needs.

f) Live a life of service. Be of comfort to others. Adopt a child with Down's syndrome or autism, or even an elderly inmate or terminally ill person and contribute towards daily care, dress, or medicines. Sharing without caring for rewards illumines the Holistic Happiness Principle.

g) Stop to savour the beauty and fragrance of a flower on the wayside, not caring if others will stare at you. Do not be ashamed to share with your inner self, God's beautiful and bounteous creations that bring joy and peace to the heart. Go ahead and appreciate them.

h) Go vegetarian. Do your bit to abjure from violence and bloodshed.

And ...

Enjoy the beauty, and the fragrance around you. Most often in life, we fail to appreciate the little joys that'll go miles and make us happy. We are afraid to bring out our emotions because we wonder what others will think of our behaviour. Societal behaviour has become rigid and formal in ways that set us aside from nature. What would happen if your boss saw you sniffing a flower? He would think you were silly wouldn't he? Can you recall in your senses the fragrance of a fresh wet lily? All you get to smell all your life is your toilet soap. So get ahead, enjoy the beauty and the fragrance around you.

Develop and carry on a life of service. Be of comfort to others. Caring for others will help you in times of your stress as you introspect, and help to relax you, as such acts work within the Holistic Principle of Happiness.

Make that difference happen to your life. Have communion with your surroundings, be it with a child or even someone less fortunate than you- will make a difference to your life. Have communion with life forms around you and stay that way.

Share your Beautiful Mind.

Petal 4
Float on Your Waterbed

You did not save it! You lost control!

You bet, after you lost it and came to, you felt ashamed of yourself. You really thought you had better control over yourself, didn't you?

You don't want to feel guilty about something you never really intended to do. You don't want to lose your temper but there you go again. That's exactly what you've been doing all these years! Your heart has forgotten its art of pumping slow. You keep pushing it fast forward with that red hot temper you are famous for. Do you know that each time you fume and fret, you are walking on the edge, ready for the brain stroke, or a massive infarct?

Every time you lose your temper, you are unconsciously preparing for the worst you could get. A quick leap in your blood pressure gets hold of you like your blood is a sudden race horse berserk on the leap tracks. But that's the last thing you want to happen to you when you could use your time to calm yourself. Don't forget your goal in life. Your goal in life is happiness within the Holistic Happiness Principle. Be ready to be happy. Not to lose your temper.

One of the easiest things you can do is to lose your temper. You lose it before you even realize that you lost it. It works almost like a reflex, often taking you by surprise. Yet contrary to popular belief, it is not at all hard to hold your temper, and keep it to yourself. You can tame your temper like a pet. Sure, you can do it. Just when you feel anger mounting inside you, check out the Happiness Principle. Get back and sink quietly into your slow breath. Make your breath your waterbed.

There is no need to boost your ego from zero to one hundred degrees flat in one second just because somebody, somewhere, came over to hurt you. Remember that just as there are people affectionate and kind and willing to help you, there'll also be people wanting to hurt you. But that is no reason to fume and fret. By keeping your temper in its grid you are not being inferior to anybody. You are, by doing so, actually maintaining your energy reserves in great shape. Not losing your temper in the face of odds leads you to sublime victory of the self and humbles your opponent who tried to hurt you. It leaves your opponent embarrassed when you are calm and don't give him a chance to make you vulnerable and break yourself. You become a hero before your inner self.

Here's the story that'll help you to keep your temper and not blow it. As I experienced it, it is the greatest lesson on the winning side as to how one may keep one's temper safe, for better use and in deep cold storage.

A thin and lanky man well dressed, but looking very distressed, boarded the waiting train at 10.21 a.m. He saw to his chagrin that the compartment was full. There were no seats as far as he looked around. But upon one of them were two pieces of travel baggage. The train was scheduled to depart in another one minute. The man went over to the seat with the baggage and turned and shouted 'Anyone who owns the baggage on this seat?' There was no answer. The lanky one persisted, more stubborn in his enquiry, seeing that there was no one to respond. He then went swiftly over, and pulling out the baggage removed them and put them carelessly in the aisle (which was again not a polite thing to do as he could very well have put them on the rack overhead). Thereafter he promptly went over to the seat and sat down. Those of us watching felt a time bomb ticking away. The owner of the baggage would soon come in and there would be a scene for us on Monday morning and it wasn't just going to be on TV. It was going to be here right in front of us. It was now 10.22 am and the train slowly started moving; there was no sign yet of the owner of the luggage. Suddenly a Lothar look alike stomped in with a coffee cup in his hand. He was bald, giant muscled and he had the expression on his face of a Joe Frazier who had just boxed out Mohammed Ali. He came in and found his baggage kept on the aisle. He stared a moment at them in the wrong place. We held our breaths. It could just be moments before the thin man seated where he had placed his baggage was pushed up, shaken and squeezed like a mouse and thrown into the rails. *But* what actually happened was marvellous. The hefty man smiled at the man seated next to him, politely requested for a little bit of seat there, and sharing the wee bit of seat in the corner sat down as though nothing had changed. The behaviour was fantastic. That was one of the finest behaviours and perhaps the greatest possible example of the nullification of the human ego that I had ever watched in the forty years of my life.

The scene overwhelmed each one of us in the compartment. Perhaps some who thought it over had a sterling lesson to learn from that unique, tranquil behaviour of the giant muscled Lothar look alike. The lesson was simple. *The ego was not all important.* The inner power of the self over anger and discontent lay in its ability to be naturally spontaneous and let the ego just fade away.

How was it that the hefty man who could easily have punched the thin man and tossed him overboard had opted to occupy his seat without a fight while choosing to sit in a fraction of a seat and simply carry on as though trifles would never be a bother to his big heart? He was so calm, that it looked as though he had used his muscles in the right direction- *to squeeze his ego to nothing.* He was a big, strong cool cat. And he wasn't just a hunk for appearances. He was strong deep inside with the Happiness Principle within him ticking just fine. No hard feelings, no fights, no regrets. Here was a guy who was not only developing muscles. He was developing something else— Good living, that kept working wonders for his heart and brain. What had the hefty man gained in the process? Sure enough he had gained the respect and admiration of each one of us in the compartment. Sure, the guy knew how to handle his inner reserves. By doing that he had become our secret Monday morning hero.

Soon we heard the voice of the thin man with all its original power and noise gone. 'Is the baggage yours sir..?' 'Oh', said the hefty man making soft eye contact with the thin man. 'It is all right... it is all right...'

The train sped on. The Lothar- like man was soon dozing away to the train rhythm. Sure, the guy knew how to get his sleep!

Most often people react in very tense ways to most ordinary and trifle situations. Looking back, after having lost their temper and exposed themselves, they wonder why they were not in control of the situation and had made a mess of themselves. A man stamps on your foot in a crowded train, and even before you think of it, you let out heat and even create a scene that you cannot thereafter opt out of. A passenger's baggage hits your hand and spills your cup of tea over you and he moves on without even knowing it, but you are caught in your temper, go behind him, show him the coffee all over your shirt, demand an apology and will go ahead and show him who you really are. And, how often have similar situations as these, overpowered your sense of control?

According to the *Bhagavad Gita*, the elevated being is one who rises above the trifles of desire and anger, and attains peace with the inner self. Peace of mind is just another term for inner happiness that you can use in splendid ways to make those around you happy.

The next time you want to blow over because someone tried to wriggle past you in a crowded cinema hall, stop. Deal with the situation sans anger. You'll find your *stop-to –think- a-second-behaviour* sending marvellous impulses of calm all about your senses. Think of the Lothar look alike during the moments in your life when you are just about to lose your temper.

Now let's see another Monday morning picture.

This is a true story too. It'll show you the nadir to which the ego and the uncontrolled temper can take you.

It happened in a full train in a Mumbai suburb on a bright Monday morning. The ladies compartment overflowed. The train came to a stop and a middle aged lady along with her friend tried to get in. The door was open, and the friend succeeded in getting in but just then another stout young lady came and stood in the middle of the doorway. Just as the middle aged woman tried to step in, the younger one pushed her with her body and shouted at her that there was no place anymore. But the lady who wished to climb inside would not let go. She tried to squeeze in just as the train started again. As the train began to gather motion, the lady had one foot on the train and one on the platform. With a hand at the doorway, she let out an imploring cry, requesting to be let in. But the stout one at the entrance, seething and defiant, kept shouting at her, refusing to give her a little space or even lend a helping hand to lift her in. The woman lost her control, slipped, fell on her face and was sucked away bleeding into the speeding iron wheels.

How sad, but how true, that often, the rigidity with which we let our ego and temper rise and rule us, we render ourselves madder than thoughtless beasts of hunger in our daily behaviour!

Where, honestly given a chance, would we place our temper in a scale of 5? If we find that we are among the ones going overboard, can we not reconsider and take steps to come back? At such times, it is well to remember the hefty giant muscled man, and how he turned lighter than an angel, with human behaviour most noble, tender, relaxed, and sublime.

Must you never ever get angry or put your foot down when you feel you are right and ought to be heard? Well, that is not the real intention. Look at the words that follow, carefully. You must not lose your temper. That's all that's been said. No one said that you shouldn't hold your temper to your advantage, without losing it. Certain situations in life really demand that you must have your say and you mean it, yes. Asserting yourself in situations where you want to have your say is not losing your temper. No two counts on that. It is but simple, that when you put your foot down and wish to be heard, as you have every right to, you ought to do it without losing your balance, and with total human dignity.

Temper, with you in control, is a very balanced and sensible affair. It shows your assertiveness, and corroborates your judgement of events which demand due respect Make your mind work for you like the radiator works for your car engine. The radiator must not heat up, but must work by controlling the engine heat to ensure a smooth ride on wheels. Give your best to your temper with just the right heat. When you are in control, you are doing good to yourself. Your blood pressure does not rise or spurt. You keep your blood, the water of life, cool. If at times you feel your heart beating rapidly inside you, and you sense your anger or anxiety coming on, you know by now that you only have to take a break, breathe easy, and count to ten!

Practice the *tension - to -calm* switch over.

It is up to you to choose between keeping your temper balanced and taking the first available leap to lose it. The first is a test of your level of competence to remain peaceful and calm in times of stress. It is desirable behaviour, and also in one's own interest in the long run. It keeps you healthy and brings integrity and self respect. Anger is defeat per se, that humiliates the self.

Reward yourself with a compliment every time you let off steam without boiling over. Let the art of slow breathing come naturally to you in times of trouble, grief, or stress. How easily can you switch over from tension to thoughts of peace and calm? Practice 'switch overs' from tension to calm whenever you begin to feel the slightest stress building up. Keep increasing your switch over speed as you go on.

And ...

Life is a circus. It is you on the trapeze. It is your life. Hold it.

Do the balancing act. Do not let your cups and saucers fall.

Radiate your Beautiful Mind with calm.

Petal 5
Heal Yourself

This is the story of the little yellow butterfly that winged its way through the compartment window of a speeding train one busy morning when the share price index was down, and the packed passengers, restless and sweating, kept clinging hopelessly to their ringing mobiles as upon dry twigs of hope. The tiny fellow, with a little left over honey still upon his curled up tongue but caught in the human jungle, landed upon a young man's sleeve. The man just rolled up the newspaper he was reading and zapped it, his face so violent as though a serpent had suddenly set upon him, and he brusquely brushed the yellow disturbance aside.

The butterfly escaped, but only to be attacked by some one else's newspaper that really got him, tearing his yellow wing to near bits An object of perfect beauty not too long ago, he was now a crippled thing, and unable to fly anymore, dropped dazed on my hand. I closed the bruised beauty in my palms, and holding him awhile outside the window let the breeze blow it all away like a hurt dream. What a sign of relief my act seemed to the passengers!

Are we talking now of mercy? Are we talking of tolerance, and compassion? Are we talking of love? Of healing ourselves? Why were we calling ourselves humans, when we are not behaving as humans any longer? What is our claim to be called Homo Sapiens, if like animals we have no sense of tolerance, pity, kindness or compassion for the life forms around us that in many ways unknown to us contribute to our planet and our living?

A grasshopper that jumped in through the train window a few days later from Cotton Green was not as fortunate as the yellow-winged butterfly. The hopper flew onto the flashy tie of a flamboyant executive. The man's big hands immediately pounced upon it, squeezing it, having its hind legs peeled off like green banana skin. He threw the crippled creature onto the ground and not just content with that act, crushed the little one under his feet with the sole of his brightly polished shoe. He then continued reading his morning paper. That is the story of the sad end of the green hopper that flitted in among human beings who are supposed to be balanced, rational, tolerant, merciful, and human!

What do we gain from the above incidents? Most of us take the life around us for granted. We don't think of the pain that we give our fellow creatures that share our world and take part in the balance of our ecosystem. What was the need to maim or kill in the above incidents? There was no motive. Though no one will ever be hanged for such acts, they still show the monstrous side of our inhuman nature. Somewhere along the way, we in our pursuit of materialism, let us admit, have forgotten to be human.

Our quest for happiness does not anymore include in its zone, the qualities of sharing letting live, or of selflessness. Being proud and selfish, we only bring with us hurt and unhappiness. Without kindness on our side, we go ahead and further our selfish interests, closing our minds to qualities that must really redeem us.

What do we really do? We hurt our friends, our peers, and come home and hurt our family and children. We then pray to our angels in heaven, bribing them with costly offerings to steal for us from God, our happiness and peace. Ironically enough, after all our bruised acts to God and man, we still we dream and hope for relaxation to enter our lives. How much farther can we hope to go with our minds that are rigid and closed? How can we be kind enough to love and care, when we have cut ourselves away from the roots of own kindness and compassion? It is here that we must realize that the truth of the dictum 'Heal Thyself' holds good for all time.

Make 'Heal Thyself' the goal of life. All the qualitative virtues of being a human will begin to gush forth from secret springs within you that you thought were not even there. Let your inner self enter the feelings and the pains of others around you, however insignificant they may appear to be. Find endearing ways to bring the less fortunate to your fold. Give your inner self wings of abundant emotion. Realize that there is no pain that is trivial, and no death, that is retrievable.

It has been ingrained in our minds through the centuries, by people who authored our religions, that all forms of life other than that of man are inferior. We have been led from time immemorial to believe that every bird and beast upon the earth exists only for us and our selfish human needs. But this is not true. Through the ages, it is the meanness of man and his inherent selfishness that have contributed to this false belief that must be corrected, to give every bird, beast, fish and flower a chance to its rightful place on earth.

Man in his inherent selfishness has gone ahead from the beginnings of his existence, maiming and killing life forms existing on the planet without acknowledging that there is a purpose and a reason for the life forms that have evolved in time and now surround us, with dimensions yet not fully discovered or understood. We gave our killings and our forms of violence upon fellow creatures the sanctity of our religions long ago. We have ever since been on a killing spree, knowing too well that we are doing wrong to the world, to our ecosystems, and to our planet.

Kings and hunters over the centuries hunted and killed the earth's fauna for sport. Believing that the fish and the shark were made for man, we have ruined much of the diversity of our ocean life and the damage done in the high seas already look well beyond human repair. Scientific studies tell us that even the neurons of fish, for example, are highly sensitive to pain, which means that every little or big fish that we eat goes through unimaginable pain to serve our palette. Now, even too late, we do not realize the bitter truth that our indiscriminate killings of our fellow-creatures have led to the extinction of varied forms of species with serious effects on our ecological balance, threatening the very future of our survival.

Over the centuries and so used to the wrongs we do in, and to our planet, we take it all for granted, giving our wrong doings acceptance, and the status of right. We have grown to be hard hearted, no more thinking of our daily inhuman actions as acts that should disturb our inner selves; remaining muted we have got used to being obdurate, believing that we become more and more human and are on the sly when we refuse to acknowledge our inner voice that keeps trying to guide us to respect basic emotions and feelings that could transform us, if only we acknowledged them, making us better, taking us closer to Godliness and the Holistic Happiness Principle. It is ironic again, that we continue to seek happiness after all the thoughtless inanities and selfish mire that we keep daily sloughing ourselves into, without hope of redemption.

The truth remains, that in spite of all the many wrongs we keep doing daily, each one of us is capable of being more infinitely human than we presently are, if only we'll stop to think and reconsider our daily acts of apathetic indifference. Just as we put to use only a fraction of our brain potential in our day to day work, we use only a fraction of great inner powers of compassion, and empathy. We really need to bring inner peace and happiness to our miserable selves, by invoking our inner values that lie stifled within us in order to try and enter our beautiful mind individually, and for natural good.

The land of peace is where we have to get to, you and I, and it is right here, where we are. But we don't really belong here unless we begin to share and feel for everything that touches us with essence of the inseparable life force. Acts of kindness and compassion from each one of us will help to soothe and lift the earth, filling it with healthy life power. Every such act will be worth more than a thousand words of prayer. Truly so, such acts shall redeem us into the deeper awareness of the self. To let that sublime triumph of our planet happen, we must let the milk of human kindness flow.

Imagine for a moment, that we are going to read adapt ourselves. We have pledged to live as a universal family, showing love for the tiniest and most insignificant of nature's creations. We are committed to doing our acts of good to the helpless and the unfortunate, however significant they may appear to be. Those of us who encounter a bird with a bruised wing will stop to help in its flight, we'll save butterflies, stray animals on the roads, help the starving lady on the road with a dime, put a limping grasshopper back on its feet, shower the compassion that Jesus and The Buddha showered upon the lost lamb...*that is the world that our Good Lord keeps hoping we humans will make of His creation some day.*

That's what each and every one of us should be doing to save ourselves and this beautiful earth. Are we getting ready to do that? Are we getting ready to let the Holistic Happiness Principle work in interconnected ways for us like functionally independent, but deeply entwined blood vessels, so that we'll be everywhere with love and compassion, hope and kindness, humility and selfless sharing, which will bond us all together, making us happy, contented, and free?

Here is a touching story that reveals the true nature of compassion.

A man was walking along seashore that had the waves bringing in starfish to the shore by the dozen, each time that a wave came up. The man kept walking, bending down, throwing all the starfish that he could pick on his way, back into the sea. This went on for a while, till a friend he met asked him what he was doing. 'Saving the starfish', he said... 'helping them get back to the sea, where they belong'. The friend laughed. You are a fool, said he. 'There are thousands of starfish tossed upon the beach and a hundred more every time the wave brings them up. Now, how long do you think you'll do it? What difference do you think it will it ever make?' Bending down, the man took a starfish from the sand and stretched out his hand to his friend. Well, he said throwing it back into the sea. 'At least it'll make a difference to this one!'

However small you think your work is going to be, go ahead and make that difference. Walk along your seashore, and pick up your star fish. Just make that difference.

And . . .

Osho, was right when he said 'No animal, is as violent as man. Animals kill but they kill only when they are hungry, otherwise not. Man is the only animal who enjoys killing for no reason at all.'

It is now time for us to insulate our earth, protect our fellow creatures and surrounding life forms in earth, water and sky, and in doing so, to protect ourselves and our future generations. It is time to heal ourselves.

Together, with the stars of compassion on our side, let's begin by holding a starfish in every hand.

Heal Yourself in your Beautiful Mind

Petal 6
Smile

Smile.

It increases not just your face value. It brightens your *life value.*

If you can brace yourself trying to impress, putting yourself confidently before something as mechanical as a flash camera, you, as a person can do much better with another human being. You don't have to fake it when you can give all you have got and smile a truthful smile. At a friend. At a stranger.

When you smile, you unconsciously reap rich dividends. A smile is a natural relaxant. First it relaxes you, while simultaneously adding to your emotional value. Your smile helps shed your inhibitions. The additional advantage is that your smile relaxes the person you are smiling to, putting him at ease and inviting him to begin a conversation. A smile unlocks the hardest of hearts.

Smile, because it inter alia, makes you pleasant and happy. Even when in deep grief, if there is someone by your side to reassure you, comfort you and have you smile, it helps lessen the burden of the tears in your eyes. Haven't we often smiled secretly to ourselves thinking of the ones we love, or while recollecting soothing recollections from memory? Your smile not only adds to your face value, it also illumines your mind.

A smile helps a person to control the tension building within. It has the power to defuse stress and anger. A man with a pleasant smile can employ its power to his advantage to bring happiness to himself and to all those around him.

When two people meet, a strange situation can occur. One can wait for the other to open up and smile starting off an 'I am bigger than you, so you smile first' game. It looks innocuous, but really the 'you smile first' game is a deadly one that can mark the end of relationships and friendships, which again is not a wise thing to do.

Be the first to smile. Whenever, wherever. You'll find that you not only did not lose out, but you also moved up to a Win-Win position, showing yourself as amenable and friendly which is all that happy living is all about. It is not at all necessary for you to wait for the other person to smile first. You do it first. If someone does not return your smile, it does not really matter. You will not lose your respect just because the other did not reciprocate your good action. Often, good actions that you do happen that way. If you can smile honestly, go ahead and smile, whatever people may think of you. Remember that your smile does you only good. You smile because you are happy with yourself, and are working towards the Happiness Principle that is radiating in your mind. If some one you see on your way isn't happy, your smile could give him an opportunity to smile back and be comfortable. Well, whether he is nurturing his ego and won't smile back is his personal problem, that'll keep on making him unhappy.

If your face looks worried and someone tells you so, smile instantly. A smile can wipe away worry from your face. Yet you don't do it. You don't smile. You are trying hard to keep your smiling lips tight. It is just as the comedian and star W.C. Fields once said, '*Start your day with a smile and get it over with*'.

Do it now. Smile. Your smile ties a beautiful band of affection, and works like an aura. When you smile an affectionate, loving smile, you help to create a glow around you. Though a smile blossoms on the face, its roots lie deep in the mind. Precisely the reason why some people can smile more easily than others.The unhappy and the scheming find it hard to smile, but they do so to satisfy their mean ends. A wicked smile lack purity, and not being born from the inner self, and having nothing to do with happiness, hangs like a loose mask upon the face. A soft, genuine smile works to flatten out ego, and usher in meaningful relaxation.

When you practice the art of smiling, take care that you are free and fair in terms of body language also. Gesture freely. Use your face, your smile, your mind and body to work to establish meaningful and lasting relationships.

Think of the wonderful opportunities you had today to smile at your peers, superiors and subordinates. Yet think of what you actually did. You got your smiles coming halfway, but refused to make eye contact and swallowed up your smiles. You made barriers that you thought helped to uphold your dignity. You did not smile because you thought that if you as much as put on a smile, you would lose your sense of respect. Are you so important that if you as much as open up and smile the earth will crash under your feet and creation will come to an abrupt stop? *Is your life goal not to make yourself happy wherever you are*? By your negative actions you go on losing out on opportunities to take part in the core Happiness Principle around you.

Do not ever confuse your self with your ego. Don't ever forget that you are first and foremost a human being. Do not act like you are an alien on this planet with higher virtues than any other ordinary mortal. The only qualities that'll ever be remembered about you when you are gone are the values you were able to put forth as a human being and the work you left behind. You'll never be remembered for the pet ego that you pat and pamper every day, all your life, for your own unhappiness. This awareness must always be at the back of you to enable you to deflate your own ego and get on with the Happiness Principle to liberate your self.

Your smile is a bountiful potion of empathy, warmth, love, and compassion all rolled into one. Only the Homo Sapien, the numan being, of all God's billions and trillions of species on earth has been given the talent and the gift of the smile. So use it. Use your smile to relax and build your state of happiness.

Here are some exercises to keep you smiling and get you into your Beautiful Mind.

a) Keep a mental count of the number of times you smiled today. Try smiling at the faces you see each morning irrespective of caste, creed or religion, or their positions in the organizational ladder. Learn first to manage people, beginning with your smile. Your organizational management will follow.

b) Try to increase your smile sedimentation count by degrees every day.

c) Whenever you come across a chance to smile, go ahead, and seize that opportunity to show that you are a pleasant person to interact with. Never withhold a spontaneous smile when you feel it coming on.

d) Watch for the reactions of the people you wish to interact with. If your smile brings you closer to people you were once distanced from, go ahead and enjoy meeting them, talking to them, smiling at them more often, making it easier to be with them. You'll be surprised how a smile can go places to make you relaxed and comfortable at points where you were once rigid and tense to be with. Not all may react well though. There could be those persistent types who refuse to smile and go on with their own airs. Do not take that to heart. But you'll be surprised to know the number of people out there who want to acknowledge you and be grateful to you for making them feel recognized and wanted.

e) Try greeting a stranger whom you have been seeing often, but have had no direct need to talk to or communicate with. Greet him with a smile and begin a conversation, commenting on his good looks, style or some part of him that impresses you. Perhaps you could talk about the book he is holding in his hands. Or the nature of his work. Or the news in the newspaper in his hands. Keep the contact alive.

f) Go ahead and smile at a child. Let it be anybody's child. Smile at the child! Sprinkle his head with your touch. Bring out the child in you. It is good to remember that children and pets are good relaxants by their very innocence. Smiling and playing with children or pets lets you shed or forget your worries.

g) Go home with a smile and hug your wife. Kiss your children. Every day. Every night. All your life. Do not feel shy to do so. This is your golden chance to be happy, so go ahead and do it. Frankly, do you remember the last time you hugged and kissed your wife and children and made them laugh? When did you last share a joke with your wife? Hard to remember? Well, when such memories become easy to remember, you are no doubt on the road to happiness within your Beautiful Mind. Start now all over again.

Begin with your smile.

And ...

Those of us who have made it hard for ourselves to smile, having forgotten the value- addition that it brings to ourselves and all around, may perhaps need to relearn to use that gift.

Practice smiling at oneself before a mirror. It would be a good act to rehearse smiling before the mirror a few times a day to confidently put across the best possible smile in public.

Make it easy and simple to smile at your friends and acquaintances or even strangers.

God could have made your lips just like your ears or your nose without its colour or blush of red. But He made them so colorful and ruddy with a reason. To smile, and make your day.

By trying not to smile, you shut the doors of your own mind.

Your smile is God's gift to you to attract and draw the world closer to you. Accept it and use it to work wonders for your happiness.

Smile. Open the doors to your Beautiful Mind

Petal 7
Spend Creatively

Look at the stories of the countless number of people pushing all their idle gold and share certificates into secret vaults and dying before they or anyone else can really use them! Some die with tons of money stacked under their beds. Has all that money on which they slept (or hardly slept at all) brought them any good?

Money definitely is a source of happiness, if had, and used the right way. Otherwise, riches are also the source of endless nightmares and miseries. We all know the story of the poor farmer and his wife. They lived a happy life until one day when they hit a pot of gold in their backyard. From then on, till the time they went back and buried it back in the farm where they first found it, all they had were sleepless nights. The story tells us that along with the comforts that wealth brings, it also brings along stress and worry that if not managed, eats into your life.

I still remember Mr. Doughdunnit. I've never seen him in a second shirt or trousers. He always wore a loose orange T- shirt which became his trade mark. He wore it wherever he went, right from the office to the walk down the end of the street. Mr. Doughdunnit was special invitee to the share holder's meets of the grandest companies around. Name a company and Mr. Doughdunnit had all its blue chip shares and voting rights. But people politely stayed away from him because they knew he stank, really. Not that he did mind. He was the richest of them all.

All his money went into shares, and the dividends were also ploughed back into shares. He had roomfuls of shares, just as an old newspaper mart had newspapers stacked for pulping. Every evening Mr. Doughdunnit sat on the ground and gloated over the splendid futures of his gilt edged papers. He did not even buy himself a chair, because all the chairs he found in the marts were too costly and not worth sitting on. He brought home wooden crates that he got free from his office, and had rags spread upon them. If someone landed in his house that was where they would sit. But hardly anyone knocked at his doors except the postman bringing in the dividends by the mail loads. From Mr. Doughdunnit's living room hung a zero-watt bulb. And that was not to be switched on without his approval. Mr. Doughdunnit gave strict orders to his wife not to invite, serve or entertain any guests, or relatives.

And no, Mr. Doughdunnit wouldn't have babies. Not even one. He proclaimed to the world that babies were a waste of time and money. They were a nuisance anyway, and would tear up his precious share certificates. There were people who spread stories of Mr. Doughdunnit's wife seen crying alone in a corner of the kitchen. No one ever saw Mr. And Mrs. Doughdunnit together. No parks, no eat outs, no cinema, they were all big a waste of money. Mrs. Doughdunnit confided to her close neighbours how much she longed to hear the feet of children in the house. But Mr. Doughdunnit was always in his room full of shares, counting, counting. The shares and their dividends went on multiplying, but deep inside Mr. Doughdunnit, there was nothing that he shared or divided. When his father died, Doughdunnit gave away his father's body to the City Hospital that paid him handsomely for his sterling service to humanity. What a piece of luck, he told his wife, that hospitals accepted dead bodies, or he would have had to pay the funeral director!

Estranged by everyone, Mr. Doughdunnit lived a life of numbers until one day, when he felt a compelling pain down his throat and so rushed to a doctor. The doctor ordered some preliminary investigations, did an endoscopy, ordered a few more blood tests, and then the results came—Mr. Doughdunnit was suffering from an advanced form of rare cancer that had quietly spread down from his gullet to his stomach, and deep into his intestines. It had been a latent form of cancer, which had metastasized, eroding him. He had hardly three months more to live.

Mr. Doughdunnit was terrified. Suddenly his share-mountain dream crumbled before his eyes. All he wished now was to have some doctor tell him that he would live. Though no one openly said so, none came forward to help him out or be by his side. Well, serves him right, thought many, 'Let his shares help him now'. No one visited him in the hospital. His faithful wife tenderly looked after him, but there wasn't much she could do, except add to her tears. He clutched his wife's hands and cried. Those three months were the only that time she remembered him touching her ever. Mr. Doughdunnit cried out loud, dumped shares in the churches, gave them away to the doctors and the priests, said he would build churches with his money, give away in charity, he would give away all his gold, and shares, if only there was hope of life, and freedom from pain. He lay on the bed watching the white ceiling from his ventilator, helpless, and friendless. Mercy soon played its gift and Mr. Doughdunnit died one night in sleep.

Truth is strange. Poor Doughdunnit, he died with all his money around him, but sans human warmth, love and happiness.

What if Mr. Doughdunnit had used a share of his money to work happiness for himself? What if he had cared for his wife given her gifts, and the babies she had longed for? What if he had come home to wipe her tears before going to count his dividends and shares? Brought home flowers? What if he had brought home friends? In the end there would have been affection, sharing, and comfort in his times of distress and pain. There would have been some one to share love! There could have been enduring moments of happiness! There were so many ways in which Mr. Doughdunnit could have used his shares to bring happiness and sharing into his own life!

We have been taught all our life that money never brought anyone any happiness. While money by itself cannot bring happiness, the things we do with money and the ways we choose to spend our money **can certainly** bring happiness into our lives. That is what money **is for.** It is not there to be stacked away in secret treasure vaults, it is only there to be taken out from the lockers and used in ways that bring comfort to us, our family, our friends and community. It can be used in noble ways to bring joy back upon the faces of our poor children, nourish the hungry, cure the sick, wipe away tears, or help a blind one see. Contrary to popular belief that money never bought any one any happiness, we can use money, to make our lives and of those around us, and those whom we feel for, happy.

It is not the intention to state here that money earned the hard way should be spent and wasted. A parallel may be drawn to the amount of food we take. We often consume more food than we need, not knowing what else to do with it- just because it is on our plates or it could be that we do not wish to part with it or waste it. Most often we end up hoarding more than we'll ever need, while aware that had a little of what we have wasted, or consumed in excess, been given away for a worthy cause, it would not have drained or caused us loss in any manner whatsoever. But we do not give away even what we do not really need, because we are possessed by our own selfishness. If our acts of our selfishness can be made selfless, our little acts of giving away to those in suffering around us will help kindle the goodness in us to serve the common good.

Once we start giving away in our own affordable ways, and in meaningful amounts, to develop the habit of giving and sharing, we begin to realize a sense of detached contentment beginning to overwhelm us and fill us with happiness. We then begin to engage in that goodness more often, letting our money work for us to make us happy.

What good is money if it cannot be used to satisfy our wants, or the needs of our near and dear? What good, if the money we make cannot be put to good use to make our lives and the lives of those that touch us, happy? We do right to ourselves when we make optimum use of our wealth by letting it revolve round the Happiness Principle of the give and take of love. The smell of money is not the fragrance of happiness. Money, by itself, has the odour of sorrow and grief.

To let money grow into a mountain heap, we often have to break our relationships, forsake the love of our near and beloved, and sink to lows that shatter the self within. The mountain heap makes us crazy and mad, and isolates us from those dear to us. We make more money, hoard more of it, think of nothing else but hoarding more and more, shut off our minds, maim and kill our brethren, our loves, close the doors to happiness, and then sit outside our mind and weep, with all the money in front of us that does not give us a chance to rise towards happiness and peace of mind. But if and when our money mountain makes us humble, it is a clear sign that we have mastered the art of using our money to attain happiness of the self.

It is not necessary to throw midnight parties in five star lounges or to fly to Las Vegas or to Cancun to gamble away your money in order to seek happiness, or relaxation. You won't get any happiness doing all that. But if you do social good, consider designing a home for the terminally ill, or find ways to feed a hundred less fortunate humans, or give your bit to the groups that care for the bruised and the maimed, your money begins to have mind value. By building up your mind value with your money, you get closer to the self, which is the source of inner happiness and peace.

Things to do with Your Money to Make you Happy

a) *Know your money potential.* Think of how much you must save to keep your reserves steady and in good order. Thereafter, think of the amount you may use for your creative spending for social good.

b) *Spend your money creatively.* By creative spending, you spend with reasonable insight to make yourself and those around you happy. Creative spending is desirable in the same manner as purposeful investment. They are two sides of the same coin. A wise man not only invests wisely, he also knows how to spend wisely, knowing well that money well spent for higher values is an investment both in human resources and for attainment of social well- being.

Here are some ways of creative spending you might try out to see if they make you feel better

a) Buy an ice- cream for a less fortunate child on the street.

b) Donate an affordable sum by drawing a cheque favouring a hospital near your home to help in the treatment of an inmate admitted with leukemia, or for a dialysis patient.

Visit hospitals, poor homes, rescue shelters, or relief camps. Find out ways in which your money can be put to use to help and share.

c) Give that coin in your pocket to the woman by the bus station in the rain begging for a cup of morning coffee. Parting with an occasional amount of money for social good will not affect your growing money tree.

d) For a change, do not spend lavishly on your next birthday. Go to a poor or sick home instead and spend time with a child with Down's syndrome, or help the poor inmates in a juvenile home.

e) Take your child to a pet hospital for her next birthday. Select a disturbed pet and care for it. Or gift your child with a loving pet.

f) Once you set your mind to it, creative spending can become a harmonious part of your life. You'll find that money that was worthlessly stashed away in some dark vault now pulsates with a life of its own.

g) Your private bottles of wine or your solitary cruise along the Mississippi with a room full of mini- skirted girls, don't end up in love or happiness of the self. They only end up with shiploads of money gone under water that could have worked better with you, without those terrible hangovers.

And...

a) Money is precious. Don't squander it.

b) Realize that money makes the world go round. Use it wisely.

c) Invest in gold, and keep your reserves growing.

d) As far as possible do not borrow money from your friends if you are not sure about repaying them. You could end up with bitterness among yourselves. You could end up losing friends.

e) If you really wish to help a friend with money, tell him frankly the amount you can offer to the best of your abilities. In money matters it is better to be politely open to avoid later misunderstandings.

f) Invest in land and mutual funds, to suit your investment needs. Invest in highly liquid securities so that you can always raise its money equivalent at short notice.

g) You worked a lot to make all that money, giving your time, your health, your precious days and nights. Now let that money not be idle. Let that money work for you in ways that'll bring you happiness and contentment.

h) Don't let your gold lose its shine in a safety vault. You become really rich when you learn to make your money work outside the vault and within the Holistic Happiness Principle.

i) Use your precious money to do something invaluable. From today, let your gold in the locker work to make you humble, to lighten yourself, and to lift you into your inner self.

j) Love is the only thing in this world that multiplies when you give it away, even while reaping you with dividends of happiness. No currency of the world can ever do that. It is love's prerogative.

Let your money work to enrich your Beautiful Mind.

Petal 8
The Wall Of Glass

As the old song goes, people are basically the same wherever you go. In America, in Mexico, in Paris, or inside The Louvre, wherever, I have always carried with me my fascination to try and understand the attitudes and behaviours of people I have come across. One thing is sure. People everywhere in this world are looking all around for happiness. But, are they looking in the right direction? Towards love, that comes from within?

Outside a classroom in Texas State University, near the stairwell, I watched a young girl holding on to her young lover, crying 'please don't go away... please don't leave me, ever.' The boy just removed his jumper so he could free himself, and long after he left down the stairwell, the girl was still crying into it, sobbing her pretty little heart to pieces.

Early one morning, while looking out of the Amtrak train window, somewhere near Louisiana, I found a young man squeezing a young woman in his arms, smothering her with early morning kisses... and I wondered to myself how long this love, that was but another name for lust, *just how long would it last?*

Sometimes my memories still take me to some of the compositions I made my fresh men students write in Flowers Hall. There were always sad true stories of jilted love. Of children looking for love in deserted homes and among divorced parents.

One story in particular by a young girl Dian stays embedded in me. Dian called her composition 'The Wall of Glass.' She wrote how she had been dreaming every night since she was three, of her father whom she had never seen, but whose love she wished she had known. The mother and father had parted just when she was born. The girl in her dream every night would climb a long winding stairway only to reach a wall of glass inside which someone sat with her back towards her, her imaginary father figure, whose face she had never seen. Dian would then knock at the wall of glass. The wall would suddenly break to pieces taking her with it, and she would fall down, down, hundreds of feet below, and wake up screaming. *All for Love.*

Late one night in Los Angeles air lounge, where it was a pretty sight to watch planes flash up and down every second, I was jolted from my dream trek to a painful sound, and turning, saw a young Mexican slap his aged father who could hardly stand, so hard, that I almost froze. The old man said not a word. The old woman by his side held his face that had turned a river, close to her bosom, and they wept together silently.

Near the Niagara Falls I watched a group of men trying to pull back a black woman crying away, 'No one loves me, please leggo, let me die,' her torso still over the misty railings.

In my hometown early one morning I saw a hefty man pulling a woman by her long hair and throwing her amidst her screams with her arms tied behind her, into a roadside bin.

In a dustbin in Washington D.C., near the Indian Embassy, I saw a sweeper pull out a dead foetus swarmed with fiery ants.

Why was all this happening? Where is love? After listening to John Lennon singing '*All You Need is Love*', why do we switch off the music video and fight? Where is love? Where is forgiveness?

I remember a journey in a train where I sat opposite a young couple seated at opposite ends of the long seat before me, hardly looking at each other for the full twelve hour journey. Both kept looking out of their separate windows and the scenery they were seeing weren't the same either. There seemed nothing in common between the young pair. There was not even an inclination by either of them to turn and see if the other even existed. In my mind I wondered whether the young couple was already heading for a divorce. *Already*?

...And there's one never fading memory that I'll always cherish. That belongs to a train journey too. There was this aged couple sitting before me, and nearly all through the fourteen hour journey from morning to night they were holding each other's hands—never for too long letting go! I stared, immensely fascinated at the pair of aged hands of the couple clasped together. If ever they let go, the hands came back with blind affection and the fingers entwined again, much like an involuntary action. It was as if they were parts of the same being that could not exist differently. There was no wild embrace, no celluloid romance, no deep squeeze, no lusty kiss upon the lips, but it was clear that love in their hearts to stay, working its magic quietly and lovingly. It made suddenly me wish for the whole world to light up with a love like that. What a peaceful happy place our earth would then be!

Love offers us the advantage of total happiness in our lives. Between two people in love, there is a giving, a taking, and making of love's great monument in which the Happiness Principle is ever at work. But yet, most partners we meet or see are hardly partners in steadfast love for life. We live in a changing world where we change love like the apparel we wear.

True love that comes from within and lasts a lifetime has ceased to have meaning. Where there should be love and peace of mind there appears only uncertainties and uneven expectations of each other. That is why love must offer great sacrifices of the heart to bring about inner happiness.

When you find fault and make excuses for not giving or taking or making love to each other, you do wrong to yourselves. You are then inhibiting the Happiness Principle from working for your good, and eclipsing your Beautiful Mind.

Don't know, man, said Rick to me one evening as we sat watching country songs on TV in downtown Dallas. "I was reading my news paper, man. She comes over with my two children, one in each hand, and says, I have had enough of you, Rick, I'm leaving". Rick put his hand into the hip pocket of his faded jeans and pulled out a faded photograph that came out with a crumbled ten dollar bill and a credit card. It was the photograph of his two little children, a boy and a girl by the beach, smiling, with Rick and his wife on either side. 'Never seen them since, said Rick, looking bespectacled into my eyes with his dry eyes as he pushed the photograph along with the ten dollar bill back into his hip pocket. 'Never seen her since either', he emphasized again slowly shaking his head reflectively, as though somewhere deep in his mind the shock of parting had still not left him. 'She found somebody else man, the kids got another dad.' I looked into his dry aged eyes and smiled.

Why do we work against our own selves to let our relationships run us down and under? Why do we do things to hurt and wound ourselves when we can as well turn around and give love and lifelong happiness a real try?

Love is the greatest triumph of the spirit of the Holistic Happiness Principle. It is the culmination of the power of the self to rise above grief and unhappiness. Love is the sanctum of your Beautiful Mind, the ultimate in human happiness.

For love, emperors have given up their kingdoms, thrones, wealth and fame. Emperor Napoleon used to write his letters to Josephine upon the saddle back of his horse while he commanded wars. Imagine the power of love!

It would be well to remember that no love or lover was ever perfect. If you are looking for perfection in love, then you might as well not love. It is in the midst of human foibles that love must make its visible presence. That is when true love rises above the ordinary. It requires courage and integrity of the self to be steadfast in love and to find happiness in the waves of love's seas. Each tumult of the heart must not be an excuse to give up on relationships that are sacred for the happiness of the self and are meant to last a lifetime. Just as prayer requires penance for fulfillment, and meditation requires discipline of the mind, true love, which is the pinnacle of human joy, has its share of sacrifices and give and take to endure, to make love last for each other.

When was it that you last held the hand of some one you loved, just to feel the touch and for the simple joy of holding your lover's hand in your own? Do you remember? Or do you have to try to remember? How often do we kiss, or reassure our loved ones to show our love for them?

Late in autumn 2000 while leaving for the US to attend a post graduate creative writing programme, my father and mother came to see me off at our hometown airport. My father had just recovered from an acute phase of metabolic encephalopathy, a condition in which sodium and potassium levels in the body get depleted. The condition, if not controlled, leads to the onset of coma. I remember the glazed look in my father's tear filled eyes as he looked up at me from the car. The look seemed to ask me, "Will we see each other ever again?" But I brushed that thought aside, thinking it silly—well, I was going to get back home on holiday in six months.

Far up in the skies, all alone, fastening my seat belt in the air plane that kept shifting away into the fluffy clouds, I remembered the laden look in my father's eyes once more, and suddenly wished I had kissed him while saying goodbye. Would I ever be able to kiss my father again? What was the meaning of that look in his eyes that seemed to be going farther away where I could never reach him? Soon memories of my life with him as a child, as a growing up son, and as a friend, began to unroll as on a video tape, and I felt tears brimming in my eyes. What if I could run down the wings of the airplane, hold my father in my arms again, give him the kiss of my life and get back? But thirty-thousand feet up in the skies was no place to make that dream come true.

That is what happens to most of us. When we are too near and capable of giving love, and making it possible in our lives, we take it all for granted and go up thirty- thousand feet in the air. But so high up in the air is no place to love. It is the place to sit all alone and regret not having loved, when given the chance by providence to love and be loved and there was all the space to be together. Three months later, alone in an apartment in Riverside, I got a call from home. Father was sinking. He was slipping back into his unconscious state. I tried to speak with my father that night on the phone, and over the Atlantic, I heard his feeble voice ask, "When are you coming home, my son? I am going to sleep, dear, I am going back to sleep". Those were the last words that I heard father speak. That night I cried in my bed. I felt my strange longing to kiss my father return, as if with a vengeance. How many hundreds of times I could have kissed him when I was home with him. I just didn't or wouldn't do it. I packed my bags preparing to return, praying to God that my father, though sinking would... wait for me.

When I met father again, he was in the intensive care unit, drifting into a coma following a massive seizure. The doctor tapped him on his shoulder and he opened his eyelids. He seemed so far away. I looked into his eyeballs as his lids opened that had started rolling, as though they would never stop. I kissed him then, saw his eyes gaze one last glazed moment that seemed an endless minute, in the mysterious twilight of fast eclipsing consciousness.... He then fell back, his eyes, unfocussed, rolling like pin balls all over. The coma had, in my presence, suddenly gripped him entirely. It was as though all along, father was fighting back his deepening coma, waiting just to see a last glimpse of his son. Now, before my eyes, my father was gone deep into his coma. There was no coming back. What use was my love now? What joy did my kiss give him? Did he ever know? Will I ever know, if he knew?

With my father's passing, I realized that of all things in life, love and happiness should never be made to wait. If you make them wait without letting them blossom in your Beautiful Mind, you stand to lose forever. All else in life can wait. Money, possession, desire... the list of things that can be made to wait in life is endless... *but not your quest for love and happiness.* Love and happiness should be made to happen, given then and there, here and now, and forever. When one discovers happiness in oneself, the self begins to shine. It spreads its aura all around. The Beautiful Mind, kindled with heavenly light, emblazons a celestial chandelier.

I took a review of the things I had missed, and of the moves I should be making so that I would not regret giving happiness as soon and as much as I could, to those whom I loved and those who loved and cared for me. The joy of love shining back at you through the eyes of those who really love you and those whom you love, is love's sacred reward.

Reviewing my life, I saw that it had been ages, since I kissed my mother, my wife or children. I did not even seem to remember when I had kissed them last. So I made it a point that even if I did not have the time enough to spend with loved ones everyday, I would hold them to myself awhile and kiss them good night every night and even reward my children's acts with open acts of love and kisses realizing now that there was no need to be ashamed to show love and kindle happiness to those whom I loved. I found myself lifting out in heart and spirit, because I wasn't hiding anything from myself anymore when reacting to myself and to those around me, I was only going out from deep within me, calm, and true to inner myself.

The mind is the lotus on which you live like the dew drop. This is the quality that dawns in living from the mind, from within the realization of the inner Self.

Start now, and discover the sense of inner joy and fulfillment as you vow to love and be happy and enter your Beautiful Mind.

The water wheel effect.

Expectations every step of the way.

Why do we end up hurting those whom we love? Love takes us through a spectrum of expectations. Expectations like desire bring us grief, because they rise within us in the hills and valleys of our love, seeking gratification and fulfillment. In the beginning, with just love's idealization in the platonic, expectations take a side step. But when realities step in, expectations come over, putting everything else to a side. When expectations are not gratified in the name of love, the non-gratification begins to take its toll in the form of hurt. We ended up hurting back.

What do you do, feeling helpless, hopeless, and filled with resent, when your expectation of your partner fails you?

The foremost need at such times, is to open up to your partner, and tell her or him what you think in her behaviour has been hurting or irking you. There is no point in endlessly waiting for the sixth sense to happen in your partner to fulfill your secret and hidden expectations, some of which may even remain unknown to your partner. But there is a point in letting reveal your private needs, so that your partner can learn your behaviour and understand your expectations, thus nullifying your need to be hurt.

Once you open the door of your heart and let your feelings pour, there is room enough to mend hurt and to ensure that such expectations are treaded upon carefully enough, and attended to. It is necessary at times when your expectation of somebody fails to deliver, to stand back and review the situation before you let hurt take over you in a manner so as to create stress, silence, desperation or misunderstanding. Was there a real misunderstanding? Why has the misunderstanding occurred? Were your expectations of your loved one practical or in the ideal? What must have prevented the fulfillment? Was the fulfillment of an expectation so important to you, that it needed to bring about a windfall of hurt and curtain of separation in your love life?

If you have true faith in your partner's fidelity and love for you, do not let small hurts from your selfish expectations get in the way of your happiness.

Remember the water wheel. To be in love, and to be happy, let your mind at all times be a rolling water wheel to your emotions and expectations. Let your mind roll on, sieving and sifting your emotions, letting into your heart only just as much emotion as is necessary to let your love or happiness be, without burdening it, or flooding it with too many desires. Work on the water wheel of your mind to make your life simple and happy for you. The simpler your life, with more give and take at every level of your life, the more you will be able to let in happiness. This was what Kahlil Gibran meant when he said "Let there be space in your togetherness". In the space between your togetherness, you'll sit in the shade of each other's open heartedness, where expectations and desires are distanced and reviewed for mutual good, and where there is room to open each other up, talk things over, hold hands and be happy.

So take that water wheel now. Let out the excess emotions you use to build up fear, hurt, distrust, uncertainty and desperation between the two of you.

Open up and confess. Do not let expectations become walls in between your love life.

When you fall into the game of hurt, think of the water wheel of emotions to turn your hurt back into love.

Here are some remembrances for love...

Love is your way to happiness and the freedom of the inner self.

Love is happiness from the core of the self. It is the core of the Holistic Happiness Principle. If you hurt love, you hurt yourself and lose all peace of mind. Remove the thorns of hurt with the fine tip of understanding from your side.

Love needs patience and kindness to grow.

Love needs your open heart to stay with you.

Hold hands with the one you love. Hold hands to show you are there and feel for yourselves the magic of touch working its silent miracles, entering the portals of love.

Light up your present with kindled affectionate memories, reliving the glow of the past when both of you first met.

Surprise each other.

Disappear together into nostalgia and bring back love as it was in the beginning.

Do not hesitate to kiss and hold each other. Hugs and kisses are great reassurances and make up for unsaid words.

Show love. Speak love. Create an atmosphere filled with love.

And . . .

Do not forget that the world turns around for love. All our rock stars sing of love, all our films exploit love, but we aren't doing love the right way. What we need to do for our happiness, is to hold hands, hold hearts, and work our way to happiness and love through the miracle of touch.

Take love by the hands, and into your hearts.

Let love in. Deep, into your Beautiful Mind.

Petal 9

Make Love with Eyes Wide Shut

The moon is shining white.

Fifteen years back, on your wedding night, both of you walked down hand in hand, lay on the grass bank and made great love under the stars. Now the night looks inviting as ever.

The river bank is wet and grassy.

Tonight you watch the moonlight upon the river bank, close the window, and go to your bed. You lie down wondering where love has gone. A few minutes later your wife walks in. She lies down silently turning to the other side. You switch off the bedside lights wondering again, where has it all gone wrong?

Will love ever come back again?

Will you ever make love, with love for each other, like you once used to?

Rest assured, you will. You can do it just like you used to do it twenty-five years before. Try tonight. If only you'll give that second chance a real try. If only you'll take that first step. If only you are willing to reach out and touch.

Relationships snap everywhere, but life is all about putting the pieces back together, without hate. If you need to have a happy life, be in love with each other first. Do all that you can and must, to show your love. Once love becomes a reality rather than just a promise made to be broken, it leads you on to the serenity of sexual fulfillment, where you can immerse yourself totally, refresh yourself, and come back to love again.

Love expects that you are genuinely interested in each other, both in mind and body. The more you are interested in each other, the more you'll understand each other's mind and body needs. That's how your sex life gets to be an ecstatic affair for both of you. Just how fine your sex life is going to be, will be determined by the way you fulfill each other's emotional needs, and the ways you enter each other's minds before you try to enter each other physically.

When love is in and around you, you may take the liberty to enjoy sex in traditional, innovative and creative ways. In fact, as the years pass, you might want to make sex more creative than ever, as, it could happen that routine sex tends to waning of sexual interest between partners, much like a repeat time-table. Partners, as they get older and more attached to each other, need to explore and discover interesting methods of union in bed, and try them out creatively.

To have heavenly sex, first be in love. Without love, sex is a cheating game. It is like skinning love alive, and exposing the body to inner *hurt, hurt, and hurt*. Without love, sex leaves us guilty, and the bodies beat a hasty retreat after the act. Sex without love is not in truthful interest of a lasting relationship. It is like mushroom life upon deadwood, after the sudden rains. Sex with love embodies in it the Holistic Happiness Principle and appears with a divine quality. It is the nearest thing to heaven that true lovers can get. Sex is the honey in the chocolate of love. With love, sex reaches heights of dizzy ecstasies.

Happy partnering is also about being honest and trusting each other, opening up, getting closer to each other with every passing day, saying no to infidelity, and letting your life- flow come back to you, with love like it was in yesteryears when her lips used to remind you of wild red cherries. That's how sex gets lovely in love.

True loving must admit to a great deal of freedom between partners, to initiate, or take to sexual fulfillment without blame, shame, or guilt. A partner's individual needs, desires, and wants in bed should be welcomed by the other, and encouraged, to make sex healthy and its fulfillment possible. There must be total disclosure of each other's body needs, mutual acceptance, and willingness on the part of partners to fulfill each other's individual and personal needs with understanding and care. Creating the right atmosphere and acknowledging each other's needs in love contributes to, and encourages total loving.

Some of the creative approaches to sex include maximization of the use of the lips, the tongue, the fingers, foreplay, sexual talking while making love, mutual exploration and discovery of private zones of arousal between the partners themselves. Of course, partners can think up their own creative ways with mutual consent that appear pleasurable and enjoyable to each other. Other ways to innovate in sexual loving include enjoyment of sex games with mutual consent, confession of individual zones of arousal to each other for increasing sexual joys in bed, giving each other delightful sexual surprises, extending foreplay, delaying culmination, talking in bed, after play, or even engaging in fantasies. Of course, the possibilities for endless loving are limitless with true love.

In both love and sex, the trifles of uneasy expectations of each other must not also be allowed to become stumbling blocks in the way of happiness. Dissatisfaction in sex clearly leads to frustration, sense of insecurity, and loss of inner peace. We should not create taboos for ourselves and end up negating our partner's sexual happiness and contentment. I remember a friend once telling me that his wife would not engage in fellatio with him though he very much wanted to, because she thought it was prohibited in the Bible. He wished to know what I thought about her views. He was not the only one who told me the like story. There was another friend of mine who said that he did not even have the courage to ask his wife to do the oral act for him because he feared that she was too much of the nun kind to admit that thought into her life. He feared that even speaking to her about it could mean his divorce. Sadly both my friends keep leading frustrated sex lives because their sex lives aren't meaningful to them at all. But worldwide, today, there is nothing believed wrong in oral play. In fact, fellatio is not considered unnatural sex at all.

The ancient texts such as *The Kamasutra* have admitted oral play as a practice engaged by even queens and kings in times of heightened sexual arousals. In modern day books offering insights of sex techniques, oral play and its practice is held in esteem and as a healthy practice. It is believed to be extremely useful as a method of foreplay among partners to arouse and motivate themselves to heightened states of sexual awareness and pleasure, as sexual organs are in fact crowded nerve heads of ecstasy. In fact, the advantage in engaging in oral play is that lovers begin to respect their bodies not just for themselves, but for their partners as well and ever more than before. A clean body keeps away from potential life threatening diseases of the reproductive system. It also acts as a mind cleanser. I remember telling my friend whose wife referred him to the Bible that he should talk the matter over with his wife, and convince her that where the mind and body are healthy and hygienic, one may engage to 'total loving' that includes a great deal of sexual foreplay and after play without guilt or fear. Nowhere in the Bible has it been said that fellatio and its counterpart are wrongdoings between healthy loving partners consummating their married love.

Good wholesome sex binds love like an adhesive, and is a miracle maker. Healthy sex acts as an effective cardio vascular motivator. In men over forty, the sexual act, as advised by doctors, helps ameliorate the problems of an enlarging prostrate. A happy sexual life alleviates post menstrual tension in women. Women find hassle free sex life following the post menopause phase pleasurable. Contrary to popular beliefs, sex is also possible under medical advice during the various stages of pregnancy. Such sex in fact contributes to 'readying up' of couples to parenthood, and helps to bond with the awaited child.

Contrary again to popular thought, couples may engage in healthy sex during the menstrual cycle of the woman. Safe, happy sex promotes a state of wellbeing that helps to calm the nerves and relieve the mind of worry and stress. A person whose sex life is happy is a contented man. His attitude is positive in his home, work atmosphere, and towards his children, and surroundings. Stable buoyant sex works in reinforcing ways to reduce stress, and is both a physical and mental relaxant to both the partners.

Most of us seem to forget that sex, like love, happiness, and good food, must be enjoyed in peace and without inhibitions, because the fulfillment of such pleasures gets us closer to relaxation and good health. If my friend had his share of happiness with the kind of sexual activity that he needed, he would not be brooding over it during office time, wishing he had met other some angel who would have given him his share of sexual fulfillment.

Dissatisfaction in sex clearly leads to frustration, and sense of insecurity, coupled with loss of inner peace.

A relatively overlooked fact that needs closer study is that sexual involvement between partners in tender loving ways can actually contribute to bring back lost love. Wholesome sex has the power to bring life to dying love and to heal a partnership back into love. Use the power of sex in tender soothing and loving ways to bring back nostalgia and memorable moments of a gone time, to bring back happiness and to recover lost love.

And ...

1. Do not lose interest in your love life. Find innovative ways to keep the zest for sex alive till your last breath, however old you are.

2. Set the playing field. There is nothing taboo in adult sex, sex dreams, or fantasies. Foreplay, oral play, hand play, after play, and all other kinds of play with each other's willingness are only natural.

3. Immerse in 'Total Loving'. Fantasize, emote, explore, consummate, then come back graciously for your partner, and begin all over again.

4. Wake up to nostalgia. Revisit old love spots and relive the old joys. Revitalize your memories and make them happy realities again.

5. Make love like it is your last night. Extend or delay sexual consummation to let your partner team up with your frequency. Start again if you feel your that lover has not climaxed (this will pay great emotional dividends in the form of love because it shows that you care a lot for your partner). Re-arousal by oral play, slow masturbation,

lingering fore play, after play, talking sex during love making, are methods to get your partner going with you.

6. Your sex life is precious like your sight. Do not lose it.

7. Make the first move. Do not wait passively for the other to initiate you. Open up with your partner whenever you feel like love.

8. Men really love women to start it all off. Begin tenderly. Show him that you can start a good game going.

9. Whenever you make love, put all your love into it.

10. Keep talking to each other when making love.

Enter your Beautiful Mind. With love.

Petal 10
Baby-Breathe

What is Baby- Breathing?

Are you breathing slowly, are you breathing deep, are you breathing right?

Most of us breathe wrong. All our lives. Shocked? With stressful living at the office, commuting to work and back, while doing exercise, or before TV at home, we engage in the act of breathing the wrong way. Most of us unconsciously engage in 'Chest Breathing' which is a shallow form of breathing that does not let in enough air deep into all of our lungs as we ought to. Even when we are told to relax and breathe easy, we are unaware that we must do the right kind of breathing that fills our lungs entire, which will help us to be abundantly oxygenated and relaxed.

Watch babies breathe. Breathe like a baby.

How must we breathe right? To breathe right, we must watch babies breathe. Watch the baby's stomach rather than the chest move up and down as he inhales and exhales. Babies breathe spontaneously and naturally, the relaxed way, by using the diaphragm between the stomach and the lungs. Observe that the chest moves very little, but that the stomach moves up and done in slow, regular rhythmic manner. Inhaling and exhaling with the stomach is called 'Diaphragmatic Breathing'.

Diaphragmatic breathing is the correct and healthy way to breathe.

Slow relaxed diaphragmatic breathing helps shed stress. When we are anxious, our breathing becomes rapid and shallow. With repeated rapid chest breathing, we bring on strain to both the heart and the lungs. With fewer intervals during each breath, the strain gets harder for the heart. Slow, relaxed diaphragmatic breathing helps expand the lungs entire, and extends the periods of rest between each breath, contributing to higher and a more oxygen filling intake while also providing adequate rest to the heart and the lungs. Air circulation in the blood improves, leading to overall relaxation. Slow relaxed breathing helps normalize high blood pressure.

Practice diaphragmatic breathing. Let your stomach move, rather than your chest. Here is how you should go about it. Lie on your back in a relaxed manner. Relax your stomach muscles and inhale deeply into your stomach. Exhale slowly and fully. Practice your diaphragmatic breathing till you sense that it is occurring naturally to you. If you breathe rapidly, you trigger stress responses in your brain. Go slow. By slowing down your breath you help relieve your own stress, lower your blood pressure, and find yourself more energetic and refreshed.

Whenever you feel yourself losing control, breathe easy and buy yourself some time. Follow your breath. While you follow your breath, whisper to yourself any of the words that'll help you relax, such as peace, calm, meditate, God, relax, joy, breathe, 'OM', sedate, tranquil, *shantih*, and so forth, while you breathe. Let the word you have chosen be a mantra that you'll use while you breathe deep, inhaling and exhaling slowly and softly. You'll soon feel on surer, relaxed ground. You'll also find that you are able to deal with stress situations evenly and squarely.

Slow diaphragmatic breathing is a practical proposition not only while you are at work in your office, but also when you are at home with your family and children.

Teach your family members, those in the office, and your friends, the powers of slow breathing. Tell them how and why slow and relaxed breathing contributes to relaxation and the Holistic Happiness Principle.

Practice slow breathing on a daily basis. You can practice it anytime, anywhere, and whenever you choose want to relax. Even while driving! Breathe deep and drive for a change. It is as easy as Kegel exercises, even easier.

Think up possibilities on your own to make excuses to give yourself slow deep diaphragmatic breathing. If possible, breathe slowly, deeply like a baby twenty-four hours a day- every day for the rest of your life!

A good way to take yourself away from work stress and attain relaxation is by going off and on into the '*Switch off, Switch on*' mode while you are at work. This means that when you feel yourself reach thresholds, just close your eyes, breathe deep and slow, try to get into a nil thought position, be there a second or two, and then open your eyes. You need to repeat three to four times and get back to work again. Getting into the 'Switch off mode' helps you to relax and get back refreshed. Breathing slow helps your lungs, your body, heart, and brain, pumping them with more oxygen absorption. The 'switch-off switch on principle' is not only a proven heavy duty stress buster, it also helps relieve computer fatigue as also eye strain. It would be worthwhile and healthy to sit back and give yourself a few minutes everyday, slow breathing your way out of work related stress. It is the wisest investment you could give yourself... *for the rest of your life!*

Breathe like a baby.

Petal 11
Sleep-Lights

Sleep? Yes, naturally!

Sleep is a great physical and mental rejuvenator. Most of us have heard of puzzles getting solved or mathematical and scientific Eurekas coming up solved in sleep or in dreams, while they held no clues, whatsoever, in listless states of wakefulness.

Sleep is the mind's way to relax both your body and brain. We all need sleep. During sleep, our conscious world is shut from our minds. The brain needs that interval to sort out events and to let us rise refreshed again.

While you are in slumber, the brain continues your work that it cannot and shouldn't be putting off. The brain works by storing data and encoding memory, while keeping you suspended and unconscious of all the trouble it is taking for the sake of overall well-being. Much like your loved one, the brain at work during sleep time, sets things in order, and tidies up, allowing for your growth and development.

Look at babies. They sleep and grow. The baby that does not get sleep is visibly irritated, tired and restless. It is also weak and prone to infections. When we tell our loved ones to sleep tight and get well soon, we are literally telling them the truth. We actually sleep and grow to be what we are. Our sleep is repair-time for the cells in the brain and the body. Healing gets faster.

Frankly the truth is that we need our sleep. Losing sleep isn't at all the right way to get away. If you are relaxed in mind and body, sleep comes to you naturally.

Sleep provides an automatic shut off to your stress trigger. In your sleep, unknown to you, you once again breathe naturally, like a baby. That's one good reason to lie back and sleep. Another is that sleep also makes work easier for your lungs, your heart and brain.

Here Are Some Ways to Get you Into Sleep Quickly.

a) Have a positive attitude towards life. Your modes of behavioural relaxation are factors that contribute and deeply influence your sleep pattern.

b) Do not be anxious or angry before going to bed. Be gentle to yourself at all times. Hold a pet, or your child and talk lovingly to those around you before going to bed. Engage in slow deep breathing until you feel yourself relaxed enough to lie down.

c) Put on an eye mask. Get into bed, turn down the lights if lights bother you, or if some one else needs the light, put on an eye mask, or even get a kerchief around your eyes.

d) Do not force yourself to sleep. Do not try to force yourself to sleep. Try and woo sleep to you naturally. You don't even have to think about it twice.

e) *The Deep Blue Misted Mountain Valley Effect.* Be comfortable on your bed. Switch off the lights, and close your eyes. Take a few slow deep breaths, and imagine a dark blue misty mountain valley with dark hills cascading all over. Add to it the soothing sounds of a waterfall. Be engaged in your blue mountain valley while listening with your inner ear for the sounds of the waterfall. Wake up refreshed, and be thankful that you dreamt up your deep blue misted mountain valley.

f) Follow your breath. In a dark room, close your eyes, and gently follow the movement of your breath. Do this for a while, and let your thoughts gently drift away into vacuum.

g) Cuddle your loved one. Lying down to sleep cuddling your loved one, or breathing your partner's body fragrances, help you to soon drift to sleep. That happens because a sense of togetherness or feelings of love are great sleep makers.

h) The meal effect. Take a light meal before retiring to bed. Avoid chocolate, sugar and heavy starch foods before going to bed. A heavy meal upsets your digestion, disorients you, and disturbs your sleep. A light balanced meal is best suited for supper time.

i) Don't go away the drug way. Avoid excess alcohol, coffee, chocolates and tea. Sedatives may work initially, but you'll soon need more and more, and they also become habit forming. Sleep drugs also tend to alter and deplete your energy reserves. Marihuana is believed to be a relaxant, and useful both for meditation and sleep with apparent neuro-protective effects, and no proved neurological deficits or toxicity with human use. However the manner of its recreational intake by smoking and its consequences on long term lung health are still being debated.

j) Have music and fun. Listen to some tranquil music before going to bed, or read the fun and cartoon strips in the newspaper.

k) Stretch awhile idly in bed, yawn, get out, talk to your inner self, or walk around your bed three to four times and roll back in. Close your eyes and think of sleep coming on. Or think that you are dreaming in sleep, and go ahead and dream your pet dreams or pleasant dreams you recollect. Auto suggestion works for sleep.

l) Do mild aerobic exercises. Do not layer them too close to sleep time.

m) Take your daily walk for twenty to thirty minutes. A relaxed ten minute walk before getting to bed often helps. If possible, get to walk by the seaside. The cool breeze and soothing sounds of the sea waves have a lulling effect that helps induce sleep waves.

n) Let your room be dark, when you retire for the night. A dark room alters brain chemistry and induces sleep. Imagine nature sounds or the sounds of waterfalls. Think of dark forest overgrowths, and your pet dreams. Feel yourself go to sleep.

o) Lie on the bed and mentally hear the lullaby you most love to hear, and preferably in the voice of someone you love or whose nearness you cherish.

p) Gently try to tap yourself to sleep. Do a lullaby for yourself, gently tapping your thighs, or your shoulders. Try cozy positions in which you find yourself when you wake from peaceful slumber.

q) Let your bedroom be a well ventilated one.

r) Do not consume alcohol late into the evening if you are thinking of a good night's sleep as alcohol can dehydrate you, or wake you up frequently with an uneasy bladder.

s) Spread floral sheets on your bed if you like to have a sense of dream sleep.

t) If you feel cold, put on your socks.

u) Sleep on a water bed if you can get one.

v) Sex in bed helps in getting you a nourishing sleep.

w) Before you start off thinking that you have insomnia, try checking your diet before sleep. Serve yourself more vegetables and fruit, and making do with half meals for the night.

x) Do not smoke prior to going to bed. Nicotine can affect sleep patterns. Nicotine craving builds up during your sleep, forcing you to get up at shorter intervals and reach out for the stub and the lighter.

y) If you feel you are not getting adequate sleep, check back on your life style and change activities to those that'll contribute to and are favourably disposed to sleep.

z) Try and create a timing schedule for getting to bed and waking up. Stick to the schedule.

zz) Make your own sleeper's diary. Note down your favourable sleep patterns, favourite sleep inducing scenery, or landscapes, sleep rhythms, and other factors that give you sleep and those that do not. Pick up and underline the factors that make your sleep easier faster and deeper. Try out those factors more often to get your sleep.

zzz) A hot bath before retiring to bed helps.

zzzz) Don't let wild and unnecessary thoughts knock at your mind's door. If you are a writer, keep a pen and your diary close by to write out the thoughts that come in, so you that you can temporarily clear them from your mind.

zzzzz) Counting sheep is tedious. Better not try it.

zzzzzz) Get into postures favourite and intimate to your body when in sleeping position.

zzzzzzz) As always, do not be anxious, stressed, or guilty.

zzzzzzzz) Be hygienic, and let your life be well sorted, and a tidy affair. When things are in place, your mind is in a comfort zone rather than in a restless frame. A mind with reasonable comfort zones is better equipped to reach a state of natural sleep faster.

zzzzzzzzz Engage in richly diffused visualizaton of colours, the kind you see coming on celluloid through camera filters.

zzzzzzzzzz) Think of rain pouring outside and recreate the sounds of rain in your mind as you close your eyes.

And...

Sleep is the harbinger of freshness. It is the embalmer of our woes, and life's blessing. If you have sleep problems, do not self-medicate with tranquilizers. Sleep disturbances could be physical or emotional or both. If your change of diet, sleep environment, change of life style, and reduced stress levels still do not let you sleep, talk to your doctor.

Sleep tight, with a love dream upon your flower pillow.

Dream, dream, dream, in your Beautiful Mind.

Petal 12
The Wings of a Mantra

It is so easy to catch your little one by his ears and tell him 'Stay quiet a minute will you?' You bet he won't. That is his nature.

Now ask yourself to be quiet in your mind a minute. Could you do it? Could you keep your mind quiet a moment, all to yourself? Well. It is but human nature, not to be quiet. It is not easy to bring the mind to rest. Some thought is always pinning us down. Worrying us. We humans just can't keep quiet. So out comes the mobile phone from our pockets after a hard day's work, because we haven't left that old disturbing thought behind where it belongs. We are trying so hard to keep our minds busy, worrying, worrying, and yet, with all our worries still inside, we are still looking for peace mind. But where do we end up? We end up breaking our hearts and minds to pieces. Every day. Every hour. Every second of our lives.

Someone said rightly 'Life is what happens when we are busy making other plans'. We are always planning. Planning, to make money, more and more money, thinking that money will bring us happiness and peace. We have no time to rest. But as we have already seen, endless money making will never give us peace of mind. We are often mistaken into believing that the material comforts we can buy for ourselves will bring us happiness. Sooner or later we realize that we have got it all wrong.

All of us keep busy, thinking of schedules to be kept, e mails to be read, and orders that remain to be executed- such that we have no time to be with ourselves. Have we missed something in not being able to be with our own selves all our lives? We have not thought about it. If we live with everything but ourselves, taking ourselves for granted, taking just our outside bodies to be our inner selves, we have missed- everything! Like the rock on the hill, we spend all our time not knowing our own nucleus- We do not know our beautiful mind.

How do we get happiness? How do we get peace of mind? Where must we look for peace of mind? Material comforts do not always make a happy man. We need to be at peace with ourselves to let happiness enter our lives. How do we learn to bring peace to our disturbed minds? We can do so by attempting to enter a state of calm within, and to reenergize ourselves with the peace born of such tranquility of the mind.

The story of Valmiki, author of *The Ramayana*, from brigand to seer- saint, and the power of Meditation.

Valmiki, the poet of India, who composed *The Ramayana*, or The Story of Lord Ram, was once a forest thief, a brigand. He plundered and sometimes even killed for a living. Here is the story of how meditation changed his life. Sage Narada once happened to pass the jungle paths where a pretty brigand, by name Ratnakaran, held domain. The thief promptly stopped the sage, and brandishing his knife demanded food and money. The sage was however unperturbed. He then spoke softly to Ratnakaran, asking him 'Why brigand, do you terrorize innocent people, not allowing them to peacefully travel the jungle paths? The brigand spoke haughtily ' How else will I satisfy the needs of my wife and children? I plunder and kill for my family so they may not starve. I know no other way'. The sage replied, "Friend, you say now that you plunder and kill for your wife and children. Go and ask them whether they'll share the burden of the sins you reap on yourself by killing and plundering?" "Of course they will", replied the jungle thief. "If they share the spoils of my plunder, surely they must share my sins too. What strange question is this you ask, O sage?" Why don't you, said the sage "bring back to me the reply of your wife? I'll wait for you to come back. Rest assured, this is the word of a holy man".

The thief left in haste to get the confirmation Reaching home he called his wife and told her 'I bring you everything. I risk my life in the jungle, killing and plundering, for you and our children. Will you not share the sins I reap to bring you food and contentment?' The wife smiled and said "Do not think I'm impolite to you, my beloved, you bring us spoils and stolen food which we can heartily share with you, but the sins that you reap, they are yours alone. Do not ask me or our children to partake of your sins; we are unable to do that."

Dazed and crestfallen, the jungle thief came back to Narada who was waiting for him. Visibly pained of heart, the brigand fell crying at the feet of the sage. O great one, he said 'So long I was a fool to believe that everything I did for the welfare of my family would be shared among us. I now realize my folly. The doer alone must be responsible for his actions and face the consequences thereof... so great is the measure of the sins of flesh and blood that I have heaped all these years upon myself that I do not know what to do...what do I do to attain, salvation? What do I do, reverend one, to get peace of mind? The thought of my sins will hound me so much that I'll know no calm or rest or peace of mind. What do I do for my redemption from my sins, O sage?' Whereupon the holy one replied "There is only one way to get the reprieve from the sins of your life. Keep repeating the name of Lord Rama. He'll certainly help you out of this mire." But how could a forest brigand and thief, a bloody murderer, bring upon himself the courage to utter the name of the pure one, Lord Rama? Narada pondered a while, and came up with a solution. He turned to the brigand. "You'll need to utter a mantra that I give you now. The meaning of the mantra will not be important to you now, but you'll realize its significance in time. Keep uttering the mantra I tell you now till I return to these woods once more. Here is the mantra. Close your eyes, be calm and keep uttering the word '*Mara*' over and over without cessation. Let the world of your body soaked in sin, dip deep into the mantra, let your senses fill its sound... Do not stop chanting the mantra'. Saying so, the sage left.

It must have been a long time gone by, for when the great Rishi Narada returned again to the forest, the jungle had known many a hundred seasons and was overgrown; Now the woods, the rivers, and the lilting breeze seemed to resonate with the sound of the words "*Rama.... Rama... Rama*" and the sage knew that the mantra that he had given the brigand when he first came to the woods had done its sacred duty. Incapable though the brigand then had been to utter the name of the Lord by directly calling Him by name, the incessant chant of the word '*Mara... mara.... mara...*' chanted continually over and over had done its sacred duty to resonate as the uttering of the name of Lord Rama. The chant of *Rama... Rama... Rama...* had become the divine melody of the jungle.

The sage looked around at the place where they had first met, but he found no sign of the brigand, though the sound of the chant of the name of the Lord appeared to be the resonant echoing voice of the jungle. The sound became increasingly sonorous as the sage carefully walked on, and soon he stood before a tall mound. It suddenly struck the sage with awe, to find confronting him, a great anthill in human form, upon the very spot where he had bade the petty brigand sit.

As the sage went closer to the tall imposing mound, he realized that it was indeed from inside the anthill that the sound of the name of the Lord kept coming. The divine enchantment in the jungle air was the sound of the thief chanting the Lord's name! So sadly shaken was he by the revelation of his sins, and with desire intense to become pure of heart, the brigand had absorbed himself heart, body, and soul, in the mantra revealed to him by the holy sage. He was soon lost in the inner depths of his being, chanting his mantra, and thus lost to the outside world. Over the years, braving the seasons, the sun, rain and cold, and oblivious of his conscious self, even as the wild ants built its great hill all over him, the power of his meditation had triumphed over the anguish of his sins...There was peace and tranquility in the chanting of the mantra and the realization of the self that nothing else mattered anymore, but the realization of the Self in the Absolute.

Impressed by Ratnakaran who had redeemed himself, the sage, rechristened him, Valmiki, or, 'One born out of the anthill'. Truly, as Valmiki, it was the brigand's rebirth... a rebirth into awakening, and enlightenment.

Valmiki, infused with a poet's heart on attainment of self-realization, went on to compose the greatest epic poem known to the present day world, *The Ramayana*, which is profound in its wisdom, and intuitive awareness. The epic narrates in heroic verse, the victory of Lord Rama over the demon King Ravana of Sri Lanka, and is symbolic of the triumph of good over evil.

The Ramayana is the holy book of the Hindus the world over.

What is Peace of Mind?

By now, we know it. It stems from the inner self, and illumines itself within the Holistic Happiness Principle. We know that peace belongs to a state of calm that must be inside us, and that it wades in with tranquillity. To create that long cherished peace within us, we first need to be quiet with ourselves, in tranquillity. When the mind is tranquill, the body follows that state of peace. The mind prepares. The body follows. How do we make the mind calm? By letting our thoughts, that disturb our mind, fade gently away.

What are thoughts? What must our thoughts in daily living be, if we wish to get closer to Happiness? How can our thoughts be made to fade away? Our thoughts are made up of our actions in daily life. Our actions determine our daily living. If our thoughts and actions are for the most part good, stress and worry have not nailed us down in a manner strong enough to wreck it. We are already at ease with our self. Good thoughts contribute to our sense of tranquillity, and inner peace. The quality of our thoughts- See Good, Do Good, Be Good. Some examples of our good thoughts belong to the realms of love, kindness, forgiveness, beauty, and compassion. Such thoughts lighten our minds with a soothing calm effect that affords us relaxation.

If our thoughts are of the volatile kind, we need to face our thoughts first before we can think in terms of seeking happiness in the self. If our thoughts are those that think of doing harm to others, or those that seek to perpetuate jealousy, hatred, guilt, lust, selfishness, egoism, or violence, it takes time for the mind to shed away such thoughts. Thoughts of the negative type scar the psyche that holds them, and disturb the mind with self-torment. The mind fills with worry, and doubts, such that self-cleansing takes longer.

How do Thoughts Fade Away Naturally?

We can let our thoughts fade away naturally, when we bring ourselves to suffuse ourselves with thoughts that make us calm or those that do not hurt us in our actions. When we do good, act good and are good, we are no not guilty anymore. When we are not guilty, we do not have hurt inside our thoughts or thoughts hurting us anymore, tearing us down to pieces. In such a state of mind, the heart rate slows down, the blood rush softens, and waves of energy that augment peace, creativity, and tranquility, are on the rise. We feel relaxed.

The story of Valmiki is a pointer to the need to let good enter your life in ways that will help you prepare for the sublime act of meditation. If meditation is to work for you, there is a vital need to keep the mind free of impure thoughts as far as possible. One who meditates must set into practice, virtues that bring about relaxation and peace within him in his daily living. One needs to be good from inside, permeating goodness all around. Qualities such as compassion, tolerance, and sharing, need to be practiced continually, before, alongside, and after meditation, to ensure a wholesome healing effect on the mind all day. It is all the more important to keep in mind that it is never enough, to just close your eyes a few moments, and then come back to irritability, short temper, bad life, and stressed living. To attain the fruit of meditation, the values that bring forth good from within the self, need to be prioritized and put into daily action

Here are some good thoughts to nurture in your daily living if you wish to practice meditation in a wholesome manner. One needs to internally encourage thoughts of goodness such as

> *Forgiveness I Love I Peace I Goodness I Beauty I Fragrance I Sympathy I Kindness I Compassion I Tolerance I Non violence I Give and take I Pleasantness Sharing I Perfume I Happiness I Joy I Calm I Peace I Ecstasy I Patience*

Here are some thoughts you should discourage if you desire freedom from stress and to help you towards your meditative goals:

> *Ego I Jealousy I Pride I Possessiveness I Enmity I Conceit I Selfishness Irritability I Violence I Anger I Lust I Desire I Greed I Regret I Guilt I Vengeance*

The Art of Meditation

It is good to start your meditation in a quiet place either at home or in a garden, or in the woods if there is one you can find close by. Let it be in the early hours of the morning to begin with, for it would be a peaceful affair with less noise or distractions of any kind. Maintain a relaxed attitude prior to meditation, which should make it easier for you to rise above your thoughts. Be seated in a position comfortable to you. It is very important that you remain comfortable. Take a few deep breaths, breathe in and out calmly and then gently close your eyes.

Practice for a while, the art of baby breathing. Think of a mantra. Let your mantra be any word that appeals to you mentally. The word 'OM' is a mantra as stated in the beginning that is ideally suited for meditation. 'OM' has a vibrant resonance which is powerful enough to make your concentration easier. Chanting the word say 'OM' over and over again, as you close your eyes and follow your breathing. The word 'OM' which is believed divine is said to have originated from the Gods themselves. Whatever, just utter the word 'OM' for yourself over and over and if you feel comfortable with 'OM', make it your meditation mantra.

Fix your mantra be it the word Om, or Shantih, or peace, let it linger like a sail upon your breath. Inhale and exhale quietly, and in peace, to the tranquil sound of your mantra. Practice the act of breathing to the tune of your mantra in a steadfast manner. Hold on steadfast, to a single mantra that must be absorbed by you mind and body, entirely.

Gently keep repeating your mantra, as you slow breathe from your diaphragm. Hold on to a mantra that is natural to your breath flow, and let the thoughts coming on, crowding into you, drift past gently by. Make no effort to force your concentration. Do not try to force away the thoughts that come rushing in. Keep to your breath, and the resonance of your mantra. Let your passing thoughts fade away on their own, while your mantra emerges, purified and calm, taking you deeper within you.

You must be prepared to be patient. Inner tranquillity of the mind cannot be had in a day or two. It is a continuous process. You have to bond yourself with your mind, and that takes time.

When you meditate on the wings of a mantra, you let our thoughts pass by, and move on in your mind, to that tranquill space in the inner recess that is free of all worry, sorrow, and the desires of the ego. The mind space sans thought is the free zone of tranquillity. It is the zone of natural relaxation that has restorative and revitalizing benefits for both the mind and the body. Keep repeating the chant till it envelopes you and you merge into your mantra.

Hold your mantra to yourself and respect it at all times. Engage in the process of the inner contemplation of the self or meditation everyday. When your meditation is through, inhale and exhale slowly and deeply and come out of your closed eyes, gently. Continue your meditation, and extend your meditation period by degrees, with an aim to keep your meditation going, for life.

When you end your day's meditation, do not open your eyes abruptly. Let the mantra come to a zero level. Inhale deeply in through the nostrils, and exhale gently through your mouth. Open eyelids gently, and continue to be seated in the relaxation mode awhile, before rising.

And...

The experiences that a lofty saint seeks from meditation involve highly complex philosophies of altered states of the inner self reaching out for communion with elevated levels of consciousness.

Meditating at a basic everyday level is different from the high degree meditation of a saint. What the common man in his sensual world needs from meditation is simple relaxation and calm.

At an everyday level, meditation offers material prosperity and inner peace, and affords recourse to good purposeful living. It provides freedom from stress, and contributes to good physical and mental health. Most importantly, a serene mind powered with daily meditation is the harbinger of love and works within the Holistic Principle of Happiness.

There is scientific evidence that daily meditation helps to lower the heat beat rate, thus bringing down blood pressure as well. For all those who are hypertensive by nature, the practice of daily meditation is recommended for at least twenty minutes a day. Steady meditation has proved helpful in cutting down on anti hypertensives and stress medicines. It is a good idea to practice meditation with your entire family for about twenty minutes every day. The time schedule may be gradually increased to around thirty minutes daily.

Regular meditation is a genuine stress reliever. Meditation aids memory retention, and promotes creativity and mental acuity. It provides relief from anxieties and is helpful for maintaining essential body energies.

Meditation can change your life.

Meditate your way into your Beautiful Mind.

Epilogue

Having come this far...

Is just entering our Beautiful Mind, enough?

For people who are content with day to day happiness and peace of mind as a get away from the stress and worries of everyday life, the entry into the Beautiful Mind is in itself a top of the world feeling.

But that isn't all. Beyond the state of happiness and love of the beautiful mind, lies a higher state, a deeper estate of the 'Absolute Realm'.

That's the realm where the twelve petals of your mind unite into a lotus and is in magnificent bloom, high above the turbulent waters of the lake, and in the deepening skies of a celestial aura, your enlightenment is a limitless ocean of tranquility, complete in the Absolute on the wings of a deepening mantra, whispering eternity...